A Perfect Liberal Storm:

When Executive, Legislative, and Media Enjoin

Barry Secrest

Conservative Refocus

Charlotte, North Carolina

First Edition

Library of Congress Cataloguing-in-Publication Data

A Perfect Liberal Storm: When Executive, Legislative, and Media Enjoin / by Barry Secrest

www.conservativerefocus.com

ISBN: 1453667369

EAN-13: 9781453667361

Dedication

This book is dedicated to all of our friends on Facebook and clients whose support has been instrumental in the writing of this book, to the Conservative Media which must include the icons of the day whose main and true concern is the direction of this country. We also must include those members of Congress and the Senate who have fought the good fight against daunting odds.

Last but not least my family members who have cheerfully supported my obsession and have often had to fend with a grumpy, focused Dad working long hours only to come home and begin writing.

Finally, thanks to the staff who have picked up the slack while I tilt at windmills.

Author's Note

Midyear 2009 there began an uneasiness that resolutely crept into the consciousness of a populace that was, by now, weary of the upheaval that was constantly beleaguering a formerly confident America. This uneasiness was made manifest by the massive changes going on underneath a veneer of normalcy. Corporations seemed to be retreating while certain members of Congress appeared to be looking down upon their hapless subjects with the intention of corralling or cajoling rather than serving.

Fear was taking root within the Civil Society and yet it was not a fear of global warming, nuclear war, imminent attack or even a warring adversary. No, indeed, it was fear emanating from governance which had affixed the mantle of Authoritarianism firmly to the crux of this nation and was making its wishes known by edict.

Odd positions of authority were being created within the government and manned by individuals from a body politic which held views alien to the Republic's Civil Society. Capitalism along with the US Constitution was under constant soft attack.

A critical juncture had been reached: Would Civil Society go along quietly into the darkness of fear, or would they stand up in independent defiance and have their voices heard?

Thus, Conservative Refocus was born with a critical eye on the constantly shifting political landscape and a resolve to speak out, to keep talking, and to encourage others to educate themselves and to join the conversation. We thank you for joining us on this journey, which has only just begun.

To paraphrase Dylan Thomas, WE SHALL NOT go gentle into that good night. We shall rage, rage against the dying of the light of liberty.

Barry Secrest
Conservative Refocus

Contents

Forward

Conservative Refocus

Epilogue: Year Two Begins

Image Credits

Epigraph

"Government is not reason; it is not eloquent; it is force. Like fire, it is a dangerous servant and a fearful master. "

~George Washington

Forward

The Executive

Image 1

January 2009. The Obama Era began with a ray of hope and a smattering of change.

The 44th President of the United States began his term with a full plate, but we were told: *Have no fear…all will be well.* The President thoughtfully laid out his phalanx of attack, if one listened carefully, as if laying the foundation for a road to nowhere that might end up somewhere in his fluid imagination. He indicated that with all of the proliferating hard times at our doorstep, his presidency would crown a New Age.

This New Age would encompass the problem areas of our healthcare being too costly, our schools failing too many and our energy use being profligate to the point of strengthening our adversaries and also threatening our planet.

Obama stated that he came to put an end to petty grievances and false promises, along with the recriminations and worn-out dogmas that for too long strangled our politics. (I suppose he was referring to something like the false promises of keeping lobbyists out of his administration after he had already hired a slew of them.)

We at some point expected the President to break into car commercial lingo--booming voice and all--that *if we act now we can also receive--a Pass on Poverty, which will be a thing for the history books--oceans shall recede, ice will reform and the skies above America will now be purged clean by no more than the pure intentions of "Change We Can Believe In."* One would have then supposed that it was a limited-time offer.

The newly elected President went on to tell us to set aside childish things (like ostentatious and monumentally expensive $150 Million inaugural addresses during bleak economic times). He further recounted the efforts of our ancestors in their path of hard work and sacrifice to allow our nation to get to this particular point. The President indicated that our time of standing pat, protecting narrow interests (Tort Reform comes to mind), and putting off difficult decisions had passed --meaning watch out anyone not leaning left.

Image 2

The President ruminated further for a while, but then also made an imperative promise to make sure that everything would transpire in the light of day, and that stewardship of The People's money would be held to account and that the issue of government should not be about whether it is big or small but that it works--no doubt Obama thought himself as the little blue pill for governmental dysfunction.

The issue of government, we should constantly remember, is always about being too big or too small.

The President spoke fluently on the Revolutionary War and the plight of our soldiers and rejoined all nations which had plenty not to ignore those nations on their borders who had not enough. Obama also made clear that the nations who gobbled up more than their fair share of resources, no doubt speaking to America, were going to have to mend their ways. I should now point out that The President, most likely, missed the paralleling counterpoint of how much America produces with the resources that it utilizes--perhaps for another time--we can wait.

Obama ended his inaugural speech with a herald to freedom and his desire to send it along to future generations. We can only hope Obama was speaking to the Freedom of the People and not of the Government.

The $ 150 Million inauguration, despite the purity of its attendees, left mountains of trash in its wake. (Recycling we can believe in, no doubt). Obama's inaugural address was a thing of artificial, teleprompted beauty. We could only wonder if his presidency would mirror his inaugural speech. The speech ranked second only to President Ronald Reagan's inauguration in that over 37.8 million were transfixed in front of their televisions, in addition to those who preferred to witness the spectacle in person. Most, if not all, who viewed were likely wondering "what next?" The answer was not long in coming....

Two weeks after the flowery, democracy-inspiring speech--where the President espoused a reverential appreciation for freedom and American values--Obama attacked Conservative Rush Limbaugh for espousing an opinion that differed from his own.

And so it began...

The Legislative

Image 3

In the midst of uncertainty, change, and a floundering economy (along with the demise of the auto industry, banking, the housing industry, etc.), at least one particular group of individuals felt quite bullish about their circumstances: The Democratic Legislators in Congress--a group that has, admittedly, never been known for its pensive frugality.

The Economic Stimulus Package was signed on February 13, 2009--a date that might live on in infamy as the Pearl Harbor of America's economic downturn. One can just imagine Nancy Pelosi, flight goggles steamy, in breathless anticipation as she flies her economic "Zero," crashing into the financial powder keg of an armory which is a large part of the massive ship that is our economy. Eyes agog, she screams, "Bonsai!" at the figurative long-lasting final minutes of her legislative career.

In fact, the inflationary surges first noted in January were most likely a result of our deficit spending--and the Statists in our Government were just getting started. The President proposed on February 28th a budget with over $1 Trillion in new taxes beginning in 2011. Most of the taxes were to come from an increase imposed on individuals totaling $636 billion. A repeal for businesses, and especially energy companies, made up the remainder of the increases.

Image 4

Obama's immediate plan was to eliminate the Bush tax cuts, and he appeared to be setting his goals to shred up anyone making over $250,000 a year—which might include many subchapter "S" business owners who were taxed via their corporate/personal income tax levels. Obama seemed to be banking on economic expansion; otherwise, the formula would have a difficult time working. Eventually, the projected 2010 budget grew to $3.55 trillion.

As the Obama Administration built up a head of steam in order to put that "Change We Can Believe In" into play, we began to hear rumblings with regard to *the type* of change our new President had in mind for us.

At the World Economic Forum in Switzerland, none other than the current Russian President, Vladimir Putin, came out in both strict and severe warning to the US with regard to our Government's seemingly sudden tilt to the left and Socialism. Putin stated: "Don't do it! We tried it—it led to our demise." He further stated that "the US should take a page from Russian history and not exercise excessive intervention and economic activity in blind faith to the omnipotence of government," noting that Socialism doesn't work and was what actually led to communist Russia's economic expiration and eventual breakup.

The interesting thing is just this: President Putin seemed to be worried--not only for the well-being of all Americans—but more so for the well-being of what is the foundation of the entire planet's economy: the United States. But his cautionary pleadings could not be heard above the roar of the brewing Executive and Legislative storm.

The transparency the President talked about ad nauseum never manifested. The President's promises to televise all meetings, keep pork barrel politics out of the Stimulus, and promote bi-partisanship had not come to fruition. In fact, the Republicans were locked out of various stimulus and budgetary meetings. In addition, the President's repeated campaign promise to allow the public to view any bill for five days on a government website before any attempt at passage proved quickly to be nothing more than pie in the sky.

The Media

Image 5

Meanwhile, the talk surrounding the finalized gargantuan Stimulus Package was indeed not encouraging. Many economists spoke out fervently against the Stimulus. The Mainstream Media, in contrast, reported with grand excitement any developments concerning the mammoth spending bill. In fact, the Media seemed downright angry that the ideologically opposed Republicans would have little if nothing of the spending bill.

But the Mainstream Media's support of the Stimulus was just one example of a never-ending stream of single-sided, liberally-slanted reporting that would fast become the hallmark of this Administration's tenure.

This was just the beginning.

Executive, Legislative, and Media enjoined to create One Voice, a singular force railing against the very fabric of this country. Thus, the Perfect Liberal Storm was born and continues to ravage the foundation of this country with an apparent agenda to render the United States unrecognizable…and more vulnerable to forces within and without than ever before.

Image 6

One Voice Is Not Acceptable. The People Must Be Heard.

Image 7

Conservative Refocus developed in direct response to the trifecta of terror that is the union of our current Executive and Legislative branches of government and the Mainstream Media.

In the midst of Constitutional and cultural upheaval, it became hauntingly clear that there was a dire need for strong, reasoned, and credible Conservative voices to fearlessly speak back to the mismanagement and misinformation constantly generated by the Liberal Machine.

That is our singular purpose. We invite you, the American People, to join us. Following is a documentation of our journey thus far.

And WE have only just begun.

Mainstream Media's Holographic Reality:
What Happened to "Trust but Verify"?

Week of 08/23/2009

Image 8

Over these waning days of summer and heading into autumn, the Press has been beside itself— what with all of the Town Hall Meetings, Talk Radio "viciousness," Ted Kennedy's demise and so on, not to mention the report that the budget deficit promises to be in the *nine trillion* range next year—a prospect that has produced a flurry of stories addressing this issue and many others connected to the current Administration.

The questions being asked by the Media in this miasma of often conflicting information seem to commonly revert to what appears to be "Liberal talking points."

One has to wonder if what the Press accused the Bush Administration of doing is actually being done unabashedly by this White House in sending out to the "Axis Networks" specific agenda items which need to be focused on and massaged into "Holographic Being."

Over this entire period, and with regard to the Healthscare debate, the Statists' constant overall agenda seems to be continually focused on convincing "We the People" that our medical care (i.e. doctors and hospitals and the like) is not as good as the world seems to think that it is. We have read story after story trying to convince us in editorial form and otherwise that we do not have it as good as we think we do when it comes to quality. One can only thank the Star-Spangled Press for delivering this "excellent," if not subjective, "news" whilst we are all currently dealing with an America which has had nothing but bad news followed by worse over the last 12 months. An individual need not look far when trying to comprehend what is going on.

Chiefly, the story which had been designed to sink us further into suicidal depression revolved around a United Nations report that the United States ranks 35th in the world when it comes to our actual healthcare quality, using their own equally applied rating system. Accompanying this revelation is the conflicting news that the average American's life expectancy has now been increased to 78 years old.

Interestingly, in looking at population samples with regard to this report, some very compelling facts come to mind. When average life expectancy is ranked by population size, which seems to make a lot more of an "actuarial sense" on a host of illustrative fronts, the following facts come into focus:

Comparison in Healthcare Quality of the Top (5) Most Populated Countries

Quality Rank	Country	Population	Life Expectancy	Total Population Rank
#1	The United States	303,825,000	78.2	#3
#2	China	1,330,040,000	73.18	#1
#3	Brazil	196,343,000	72.4	#5
#4	Indonesia	237,512,000	70.7	#4
#5	India	1,148,000,000	64.7	#2

Comparison Inserts:

Country	Population	Life Expectancy
European Union	499,794,855	77.32
United Kingdom	51,100,000	79.4

**Date sources: CIA Factbook 2009; 2009 United Nations Healthcare Census

As one can see, the United States ranks **head and shoulders** above any comparatively ranked population size with regard to healthcare quality. This data was quite surprising when the urge came over us to look at healthcare quality from an actuarial perspective. It would appear that in all of this data one fact becomes apparent. The larger the population size is within a given country, the more the "Law of Decreasing Returns" applies.

There were several other fascinating things that come both to mind and into stark analysis when reviewing this data. The most amusing was the fact that the European Union, which seems to me to be the "Ideal Model" for our Social Media's self-esteem problems, scores below the United States in overall rankings, although their population is higher. This appears to score an overall point in the analysis' favor when looking at my argument "holistically." The other point which "glares" to this individual is the relatively small population slice of the

United Kingdom in comparison to these other countries when noting the almost negligible increase in life expectancy over the United States. We all have heard of the problems with UK's system, but it only serves a population of 51 million. The US is *six times larger* than Great Britain, for Heaven's sake. Canada's population is even less at roughly 33 million, but they have no problems—right?

It is indeed amazing how the Press will throw out numbers, and we all must then "bow down" without applying any logical principles to the data we are being given. There are some whom might argue that the healthcare comparison to the top five countries is unfair due to the fact that, industrially speaking, the US is far ahead of its population-counterparts. To these people we would rebut that this simply speaks to the exceptionalism of America and its "Capitalist System."

I hope that at least some few will look at this analysis and come away with the knowledge that simple data is not enough. The data needs to be couched in a commonsensical progression in order to be able to actually see what is happening. I will leave it to the Pros or the Pundits to argue the merit of all of this; however, this particular data seems to be missing within the continuing debate.

"Trust but verify" seems not to be enough these days, does it?

Of Cars and Czars and Credit Cards: Dodging the Wrecking Ball of Debt, Diversity, and Doubt

Week of 08/30/2009

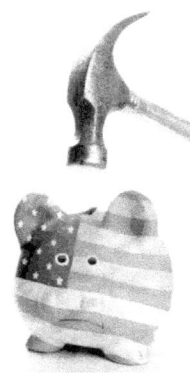

Image 9

Lately we have actually been hearing a smattering of "Lunatic Politicos" talking about the possibility of another "Stimulus." *Indeed.* Is the first one not doing enough damage for these folks?

The reason for the initial "Behemoth Economic Stimulus," according to the **"Messianic Monty Python Accounting Troupe"** in the Executive and Legislative branches of our government, was to jumpstart the US economy, which has been in a depressed mode—to put it lightly. As a result of outlaying an estimated 10% of the total $787 Billion for 2009, our economy has now, according to virtually every Mainstream Media outlet, jerked forward again. Truthfully, none of us knew that a Skateboard Park in Pawtucket or the Wild Horses sauntering around out West had anything to do with our economic vitality, but this just illustrates how the US economy is intricate beyond any plausible reason ...I suppose.

I can hear everyone clapping and whistling and jumping around out there right now. It's over, right?

Well, maybe/maybe not. According to a Senior VP at a large Charlotte bank whom I recently met and befriended, the "back pain" from all of this upheaval is soon to start. According to this gentleman, no amount of stimulus from any quarter is going to erase the continued pain that alternate industrial sectors will be feeling. After a frequently heated argument over "whom or what" actually started all of this economic mess, I came away at least enlightened that it was not "all Government's fault," although I was still able to successfully maintain that "government meddling" was more culpable than any one other single impudence brought to bear by the guilty parties.

To get to the point, the US is looking at massive deficits that stretch off into the hinterland as a result of the TARP payments, auto bailouts, bank, and AIG bailouts. In fact, the Stimulus has been like a hyper-wrecking ball when it comes to these deficits. In leafing through the CBO's estimated impacts on our budget, the one thing that an individual can take away from it is "GOVCO is spending our nation into oblivion."

Can't you guys just burn your credit cards, too? Or perhaps the US flag is your parchment of choice.

Hypothetically, what would happen if "We the People" decided that the remaining Economic Stimulus Plan were unworkable? The total payout for the bill as passed was set at $787 Billion dollars. Interestingly, the total deficit for 2009 will be $1.587 Trillion, and then the deficits will supposedly stabilize at roughly $700 Billion through 2019. Instead of talking of another Stimulus, we should be talking about a REPEAL.

At any rate, **the wildcard in all of this is inflation!**

The CBO's estimates do not take into account a wild and uncontrollable ramping up in inflation as a result of our poor economic showing, because it is only hypothetical. But the true risks we are taking in these "seemingly controllable" deficits may take on a life of their own in the not-too-distant future. If this happens, our "little wish list" spending spree could become the US economic version of "Godzilla" **rampaging through our cities,** but in this case, he will not just stick to the coastline.

In other great news, the President has now appointed a "Diversity Czar" in order to make sure that our local radio stations are "fair." If they are not "fair" as judged by a hand-picked (but extremely impartial) panel appointed by the (extremely impartial) President himself (thank goodness), a penalty will be assessed that may equal the entire yearly gross of the station in question (thereby effectively putting it out of business). Then an "impartial" FCC will allocate the license to a station that *is* fair. Oh, and by the way, the penalties that are assessed will go to **National Public Radio—long known as a...*bastion for fair thinking*?**

The main thing to remember about our current Executive and Legislative branches of government is that the determination of "fair" seems to belong only to those who have a majority of legislative votes, and in the past, "fairness" has normally been decided by our Justice System. It is indeed unfortunate that a "Diversity Czar" is not being appointed to monitor this current Administration. I feel certain that the assessed penalty levied for "Fairness Transgressions" would cause even China massive deficits.

The President should be mindful of the fact that he is the President of this entire country rather than just his democratic constituents. Since the early days of the defining Constitution, each President has been tasked to understand that his responsibilities go way beyond his own ideologies and that few men can successfully navigate through these difficult, introspective waters. But this was why a majority of Americans voted *this* particular man into the office. It is the nature of how we vote for our presidents.

This would also seem to imply that "abrupt changes" in the course of this country could cause upheavals that are destabilizing across all economic and social sectors, but to the Democrats this could be simply part of the plan. I have often thought, in looking back over the last several years, that other countries probably view our extreme political weaving from left to right over time to be much like a "drunk" speeding down the highway of political ideologies.

Appointing "Czars," a practice left over from the Bush administration, should best be left up to the Russians since they garnered centuries of experience at it, notwithstanding the fact that this practice more appropriately belongs in an Oligarchy than a Democratic Republic. If, indeed, we still are one.

A Natural Intensity Unfolding: We the People, Politics, and the Press

Week of 09/06/2009

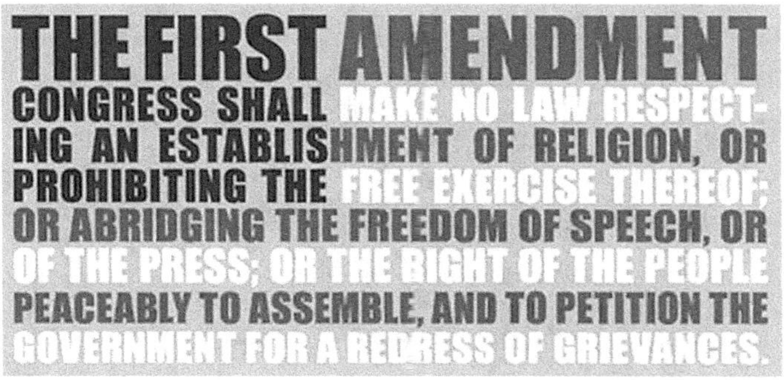

THE FIRST AMENDMENT
CONGRESS SHALL MAKE NO LAW RESPECT-
ING AN ESTABLISHMENT OF RELIGION, OR
PROHIBITING THE FREE EXERCISE THEREOF;
OR ABRIDGING THE FREEDOM OF SPEECH, OR
OF THE PRESS; OR THE RIGHT OF THE PEOPLE
PEACEABLY TO ASSEMBLE, AND TO PETITION THE
GOVERNMENT FOR A REDRESS OF GRIEVANCES.

Image 10

The Mainstream Media most recently has been in a "self-contemplative mode," questioning their own coverage intensity over these past few days as demonstrated in a number of columns, as well as a particularly nauseating sequence of verbal give-and-take between several journalists on National Public Radio. Finally! One might think they are regaining
their collective journalistic sanity?

Alas...Not this time, I am afraid.

No, the manifestation of this apparent "mind-linked Borg-like questioning" of the Media's role was not about the particular angle of their views or their own objectivity as most might think. Rather these journalists were wondering if they might be the cause of the proliferation of over-flowing Town Hall meetings all over the country against the Healthscare Bill (HR3220). Their reasoning was that by covering these "not-really-events" (their terminology), they actually caused an avalanche of anti-government sentiment against the pending legislation. In other words, the Media, in its own immodest summation of its role, has resorted to a form of "self-absorbed narcissistic navel-gazing," for Heaven's sake.

Their main inward-looking question being: "Did WE, the Mainstream Press, CAUSE all of this?"

When considering their current mind-set, in conjunction with the long-held theory concerning the symbiotic relationship between the Mainstream Media and "The Statist's Agenda," this relationship certainly seems to have been played out for all to see when looked at from a certain point of view (see Liberty and Tyranny by Mark Levin).

This led me to wonder if perhaps the White House, in a "strongly worded talking point," has purposefully sent an entire sector of the journalistic community into a spiraling tailspin of guilt for actually reporting events as they unfolded. Unquestionably, a majority of Americans would be happy to relieve these "Navel Gazing Pundits" of their neurotic guilt by loudly proclaiming "NO! You

had very little—if anything—to do with all of this."
Rather bizarrely, the Media's guilt seems to lie in the
fact that they unwittingly exposed in their coverage of
these events the outrage of the Citizenry (to itself),
which ultimately was a detriment to the Administration's
agenda.

These journalists can honestly then be heard trying to
deceive themselves, and/or someone outside of the
"Beltway Loop," that the continued gathered voices of an
America Populace, which is still Conservative at its core
and beyond, is not gathering up en mass and speaking
out in force against the radical, liberal leanings of a
president (whom was not nearly as vetted as his
opposing vice-presidential counterpart). They then
proceed to blame "corporate interests," as if the entire
citizenry were paid to attend? Now that would indeed be
a stimulus! Despite all evidence submitted to those
"trained-to-observe" journalists, they do not wish to see
the meaning in these events unfolding.

The simple truth is that the Media's reporting of an event
does not necessarily strengthen the natural intensity of
the event. The intensification thereof will always belong
to the event itself. Journalists can no more impact an
event's outcome than they can the strength of a
hurricane—both a populace and a hurricane being
natural forces.

Please. "Get real."

We can help you with that...

To wit, the "Civil Society" of the United States has lost so much confidence in this particular Administration that they have "awakened" and become actively involved in their own governance. This came about through a conflagration of diverse items: From a nearly rammed-through Healthscare Bill, which belongs more in a "B-Grade" horror movie than in the Law Books of the United States, to criminalizing our Foreign Intelligence Services, such as the CIA, while sending self-proclaimed terrorists to an unlimited vacation in the Caribbean Islands (among many other things too numerous to recount in this article).

Sen. Sue Myrick (R) NC, put forth an amendment to HR 3200 requiring the White House, its staff, and the President himself to automatically enroll in the Public Option created by America's Affordable Health Choice Act. Myrick's initiative was tabled by a vote of 36-22 (see Myrick press release dated 7/31/2009,"Myrick Healthcare Amendment Fails in Committee"). Another earlier, but similar, bill from Sen. John Fleming (R) LA, put forth a measure to require that both legislative branches of the government could not pass the Healthcare Bill without being subject to it. Fleming's measure was tabled in a Senate Committee without as much as a vote (see Congressman Fleming's website, http://fleming.house.gov). The Senators, in effect, could be heard saying, "You want us to do WHAT with OUR healthcare?"

This congressional rejection told the American People all that they needed to know about this bill. Let me point out that being born and raised in a "Let the Buyer Beware" Free Market Society does, indeed, have its advantages. How ignorant must those in power think we are?

It should also be pointed out that any Senator(s) with the integrity and courage to put forth such measures as this redirected Bill Addendum indeed have "We the People's" best interests at heart and should be celebrated and remembered at re-election time as to what is good in our government. The Lofty Legislative Folk whom tabled the measure should also take note that their legislative time in the "would-be Oligarchic Government" might be short-lived with regard to the next election. The political memories of your Constituents, Dear Congress Folk, will not be as short-lived as in years past—especially after this most intense of all rounds of political upheaval.

Dangers of Diversity Czar to the Media

Ranging deeper into the mystifying aspect of much of the Mainstream Media, and with regard to the Obama

Administration, the latest installment of Deferential Governance, which involves a "Diversity Czar," has (strangely enough) been left out of most editorial pages. We have seen several Op-Eds addressing this most concerning of items; however, the Mainstream Press has been "strangely silent" about the whole affair.

The Diversity Czar's main focus is to monitor and fine local radio stations due to a perceived "disparity" in the amount of Liberal or Progressive or Statist (take your pick) commentary as opposed to Conservative Commentary. Due to this disparity, the White House intends to make corrections for the good of all.

Now, if I might weigh in for a moment. The fact that there is a considerable lack of Conservative "viewpoint" covered among Network News and at least 80% of newspapers in circulation apparently does not mix into this particular equation. Why? Well, in a nutshell it is because the aforementioned outlets carry the Administration's' water quite well (remember the Healthcare Bill's network debut?). In "Local Radio" we have a medium which is difficult to control in that it is "We the People's" medium. The agenda is to silence this medium. In addition, the United States' leading voice, like it or not, against the White Houses' agenda is well known to be Rush Limbaugh.

Does anyone see the connection here?

Rush Limbaugh's listenership has been estimated at anywhere from 35 to 50 Million voters at varying times, but Rush is not the only catalyst here. We also have Hannity, Beck, Lewis, O'Reilly and Levin, among many others, weighing into this mix—all with a solid listenership.

The White House states that the free-speech squelching "Fairness Doctrine" that was put into play a number of years ago and later shelved is not being re-mandated.

No, this over-reaching play is an end-run around the Constitution in the form of, once again, "The Czar Initiative."

Make an "Executive Branch Draconian Post," and then trample all over the US Constitution by setting rules that play into your own favor.

The simple fact is that this practice is extra-Constitutional and should be challenged by every means at our disposal. Please refresh your memory with the following:

US Constitution, First Amendment:

Congress shall make no law respecting an establishment of religion, or prohibiting the free exercise thereof; or abridging the freedom of speech, or of the press; or the right of the people peaceably to assemble, and to petition the Government for a redress of grievances.

It is simply not the Executive Branch's job to make law. This function belongs to the Legislative Branch. It is not the Executive Branch's job to "judge fairness"; this function belongs to the Judicial Branch. Both Congressional and Judicial Branches, I should think, would be very sensitive to the Executive Branch's seeming usurpation of **powers that do not belong to it.**

Therefore, if they cannot make law (and politically monitoring radio stations is not within the purview of the law), then they cannot "legally censure" any broadcast for political content.

The rationale for this action, as put forth by the Executive Branch, is to insure fairness for the good of the People. Were I a member of any of the other outlets, I would be screaming bloody murder about the first incremental step into abridging the Media's fundamental right of Free Speech. Simply put: Any logical person knows that the first step in censure is just that. The next step may well come **into their own fold**; or perhaps they are simply too giddy to see it just yet.

"Of all tyrannies, a tyranny sincerely exercised for the good of its victims may be the most oppressive. It would be better to live under robber barons than under omnipotent moral busybodies. The robber baron's

cruelty may sometimes sleep, his cupidity may at some point be satiated; but those who torment us for our own good will torment us without end for they do so with the approval of their own conscience."

~C. S. Lewis
English Essayist and Juvenile Novelist (1898 - 1963)

Dissecting Liberal Journalism: Is the Room Spinning or Is It Just the Story?

Week of 09/18/2009

Image 11

The ACORN flap, along with Joe Wilson's rant, has flushed Jimmy Carter out into the Media to assert that many Conservatives everywhere, but especially in Georgia, are racists. I take umbrage at this implication. The Carolinas are WAY AHEAD of Georgia in that we have at least four or five serviceable tracks compared to Georgia's measly one or two. In addition, WE have a slew of both racists teams and racists drivers—probably more than any other place in the world. I would be remiss if I did not also point out that WE pioneered the sport when our Great-Grandfathers, both during the Depression and after, made moonshine and were forced to drive like "bats-out-of-hell" in suped up cars in order to evade those pesky tax revenuers from the Government (remember the Dukes of Hazard?). The result of all this was the advent of Stock Car Racing and NASCAR. So, take that! Mr. Peanut Man.

And on a slightly more serious note, we have the following New York Times story, so ripe when they finally reported it that you actually got a whiff of embalming fluid while reading it. Their three-to-four day response time in actually reporting the scandal made me wonder if Obama may be making plans to nationalize the Times and turn it into Nationalized Healthcare's Poster Boy for "First-Alert Medical Emergency Responders."

But in this story, and from time to time, we have the distinct pleasure to run across reporting from the overall Liberal Mainstream Media, which, on the surface appears to be a well-written and factual story concerning an event that is print-worthy, but is in fact written in an oh-so-slanted way.

In this particular instance, we noticed a newsfeed story in our large regional newspaper dated September 16, 2009 which hailed from The New York Times and the Associated Press.

In this story, the reporter, with unbridled and zealous Zeitgeist, starts out the slant within the title itself. The headline reads: Video Success for ACORN Opponents.

Now, if one observes very closely, the reporter has already set the story up so that the reader is focused, not necessarily on ACORN, but rather, OPPONENTS of ACORN, which, in retrospect would probably be anyone with even a semblance of character.

Why did the reporter not simply state, *ACORN Caught Red-handed--Journalists Score a Massive Coup in Investigative Journalism?* Is this not also the truth?

Yes, indeed it is! But this would skew the reader's range of thinking to the Investigative Journalist's side rather than ACORN—and this simply would not do for our strident Liberal reporter.

The story goes on to outline how "conservative opponents sought to tar the President's campaign with allegations of voter fraud etc." and explains that ACORN had worked on the President's campaign.

Once again, the reporter tries to set up the premise that Conservatives—all along—have been, in essence, trying to nail ACORN for something, as if their many and varied (documented) transgressions were simply dreamed up, and almost as if ACORN never did anything to deserve such treatment (Poor Guys).

What should have been written is the following: *ACORN has been indicted and implicated in many issues—both political and domestic—but has for the most part remained outside of any major news scandals.*

The reporter then sets out to discredit the Investigative Journalists themselves by saying: "But it took amateur actors, posing as a prostitute and pimp and recorded on hidden cameras in visits to ACORN offices, to send government officials scrambling in recent days to sever ties with the organization."

Rather than referring to "the Investigative Journalist's disguising themselves as a prostitute and pimp," the reporter refers to them as "amateur actors," which is a bit demeaning and dismissive in that the reporter omits the fact that they were **journalists "disguised as a prostitute and a pimp."**

Well, Einstein Reporter, that is often part of investigative journalism—pretending you are someone you are not in order to "get the story." I suppose our intrepid reporter missed this part of the class in Journalism 101 (probably took the day off to hug a tree or some such).

The reporter then goes on to point out "how gleeful Conservative Activists [new one on me] and Broadcasters were about the success of the tactics used to expose ACORN workers." Gleeful is a snide comment in this usage in that it conjures

"Schadenfreudian" type emotions at the expense of someone else's demise.

The reporter could have simply pointed out that *Conservatives were pleased that the imputed transgressions of ACORN had finally been brought to light.* Unless the reporter had crawled around inside of most Conservatives' heads, he would not have been able to accurately gauge anyone's level of satisfaction at a culminating event such as this, but our reporter must keep up the slant throughout the story in order to, once again, point out how "mean we Conservatives are," rather than simply report the facts.

Next the reporter links the ACORN flap with "Van Jones, a White House official attacked by Conservatives led by Glenn Beck of Fox News Channel for having signed a petition that intimated that President Bush had permitted the 9/11 terrorist attack" by stating that this news event had occurred a week before and was, therefore, "Conservatively connected."

Here, I will give the reporter credit for actually using the word "terrorists," although the White House may give him a lower grade on his report card for using this "now re-languaged terminology"—Foreign Counter Insurgents or something like that (I don't accept the re-languaging effort in that it is revisionistic).

The reporter then points out that "Conservatives believe they have hit upon a winning formula for such attacks," as if better than half of the United States' population— being Conservative— is in total and complete collusion with one another. We wish...but unfortunately we have our own specific interests and take talking points from no one. It's just who we are: Individuals with rights and all.

The story continues for several paragraphs as if the reporter were essentially worn out from all of the monumental spin effort—or maybe it's just me—but then finally in the last paragraph he gets in one more stab. The reporter indicates that "Bertha Lewis, the chief organizer for ACORN, asserted that the bogus prostitute and pimp had spent months visiting numerous ACORN offices, including those in San Diego, Los Angeles, Miami, and Philadelphia, before getting the responses they were looking for."

A more proper, un-slanted wording would be something like: ***While not denying the transgressions, ACORN spokesperson Bertha Lewis indicated that these were rare, isolated instances rather than the scandal being extremely widespread.***

But, once again, the reporter skews the language to imply that—hey! this could have happened anywhere if you hit enough places. This brings to mind the theory of random variety of serendipity—could have happened anywhere given enough time.

Once again, you can please be the judge of this, but we at Conservative Refocus believe that we have credibly pointed out how "The Statists' Media" can subtly shade a story's texture and tint in order to divert the true conclusion that a reader comes to when digesting a story. Many Conservatives have learned the hard way how to be on guard for this sort of mind-influencing retelling of events.

A Perfect Liberal Storm: When Executive, Legislative, and Media Enjoin

Week of 09/24/2009

Image 12

I suppose it is a good thing that the President has become so inclined to appear on television day-in-and-day-out ad nauseum. He is even more profligate than a rock star promoting a new tour.

His oh-so-frequent appearances have become, in many ways "nostalgic," much like my childhood days of coming home from a long day at school, playing outdoors for a time and then settling down to enjoy another rousing rerun of "Gilligan's Island" or—perhaps in this case—"Lost in Space" would prove more apt. Though one may have seen the reruns hundreds of times, they must be watched again in order to catch some subtle nuance that may have been missed or, in Obama's case, some **monumental unintended policy redirection.**

The President's constant child-like revelations of possible new and revolting consequences to the proposed legislation—when challenged—and then his dismissive wave of a hand that the ultimate outcome of the Healthscare Bill will be "just absolutely fantastic for all involved" (see Stephanoupolis interview) reminds me of author Charles Frazier's great quote: **"The words fell from his mouth much as manure from a horse, but the manure being of greater value since it can be used at least as a fertilizer for one's garden"** (13 Moons).

The **"Mystifying Messianic Megalomaniac"** has become so engrossed in appearing on whoever's show at whichever time that it leads me to wonder how he can possibly get any of the State's work done at all. Hmmm...in retrospect, a just-now epiphany: I hope that the President will make an even greater effort at appearing on more shows as often as he possibly can. There may even be a few Hollywood-types who would jump at the chance to place the Prez within his own sitcom so that we all might emit peals of laughter at his antics on a weekly basis during primetime (oh…wait…).

On Letterman's show, the President pointed out that, to date, the Obama Administration had done more to lower carbon emissions than any other administration. INDEED!

Allow the economy to remain wrecked without any sort of prodding by way of de-taxation instead of the threat of huge increases—Sir—and there will be far fewer people driving to work. Factories have closed or are operating at substantially reduced capacity, shipping is down markedly, and construction is at a near standstill. The actual question should be "how could we not produce less carbon emissions?" for Pete's sake. Your Stimulus, Sir, has only kicked in 5% of the funds to-date; that is a mere drop in the bucket that will have virtually no tangible effect on the economy, so let us not even go there! (But the wild horses out West are still very appreciative.)

If this "Green" outcome the President is touting was actually part of his agenda, then ultimately it would appear that the current "emissions reducing plan" is working like gang-busters; however, it is neither what Economists nor the American people would consider "sustainable and realistic" with regard to long-term economic plans.

"Duh."

The Statist Posse Rides to the Rescue of.....Decorum?

It has been truly illuminating to read and hear the plethora of Mainstream Media Opinion Columnists and Reporters indicating to all of us just how OUTBURSTS IN A JOINT SESSION are unheard of, **have never been done in history,** and that it is now, according to **Maureen Dowd**, a **"racist"** act. **Kathleen Parker** says, "It just isn't done—**period**" and that "in the old days Wilson would have been challenged to a duel" (talk about great television). "I don't think that this would have happened" to a White president, said Rep. William Lacy Clay, D-Mo (dare I point out?...).

"I'm a big believer that we all make mistakes," Obama said. "A lawmaker shall conduct himself at all times in a manner which shall reflect credibly on the House of Representatives," said House Majority Leader Steny Hoyer, D-Md. "The other party has been stoking the flames of disrespect among the people," and "I guess we'll have people putting on white hoods and uniforms," said Henry Johnson, D-Ga.

If I might weigh in with a suggestion to the "Messianic Authoritarians": Perhaps Congress should also consider employing facial recognition software in order to verify that none of the sitting members are exhibiting expressions that could be construed as "disdainful" or "hate-filled" whilst the President is on one of his "Oral Expeditions."

Regardless of all of this "caterwauling," Conservative Refocus has gone to some length and found a plethora of these so-called "Racists Incidents" throughout our country's 233 year history. We can only admonish these "constantly-getting-it-wrong" Liberal Columnists and Congress Folk to perhaps either conduct a little more research in order to establish some semblance of veracity or to actually read up on your employers' history (be you a Congressman) so that you do not embarrass yourselves by employing the Race Card **after a preponderance of the American People have voted in a Black Man for President** and—not to mention—the Congressional Folk themselves whom are leveling these grossly misaligning accusations (this was predicted by the way). Here is a list of just a few of these shocking events that have never happened before:

Who/What	Where/When
On the House Floor, a representative from Vermont attacked a colleague from Connecticut with a cane—only to be attacked himself with a pair of fireplace tongs.	The House Floor Early 1800s
William Graves of Kentucky shot and	The House

killed fellow Congressman Jonathan
Cilley of Maine during a pistol duel
over words spoken on the House
Floor. (Graves wasn't even expelled.)

Floor

1838

A Congressman from South Carolina,
angered by a speech on slavery,
entered the Senate Chamber and beat
a Senator from Massachusetts into
unconsciousness with a metal-topped
wooden cane.

The Senate
Chamber

1859

President Woodrow Wilson was
heckled by a group of female
protesters who unfurled a yellow and
black banner over the railing in the
House galleries that read, "President
Wilson, What Will You Do For
Woman Suffrage?"

The House
Chamber

Dec.5, 1916

Although the women sat silently,
their banner heckled the President.
The President kept on reading his
speech, but the banner diverted public
attention and captured the headlines.

Republican presidential nominee
George H. W. Bush sought to step up
his criticism of Michael S. Dukakis,

October 12,
1988

saying that the Democratic nominee was a "feel-nothing candidate" and "believe-nothing candidate" because of his criticism of foreign ownership of American companies.

But Dukakis, informed in advance of Bush's planned attack, retaliated even before Bush had uttered the words. And by the time the Vice President was delivering his speech, his planned attack lines were stepped on by protesters.

Bill Clinton was heckled by a group of Republicans during an address to Congress.	1993
Anti-war protesters heckled the US Secretary of State, Donald Rumsfeld as he made a statement to a Congressional Committee. Mr. Rumsfeld paused during a testimony outlining the Bush administration's view of the threat posed by Saddam Hussein as the protesters unfurled banners behind him.	Congress September 18, 2002
President George W. Bush:	2004

Democrats delivered a "Chorus Of Boos" during Bush's State of the Union when he called for renewal of the Patriot Act, according to the Washington Times.

President George W. Bush: Dems   2005
howled, hissed and shouted "No!"
when Bush pushed for Social
Security reform in the State of the
Union: "Foreshadowing the
contentiousness of the coming debate,
Democrats broke decorum and booed
twice," according to the National
Journal.

Is There Really a Healthcare Crisis?

Washington Post National Columnist, Michael Gerson, very astutely points out in his 9/10 article, that there is no true crisis. Polls have shown that 80% of Americans are satisfied with their healthcare coverage— 90% of those Americans with serious illnesses are satisfied with their coverage.

Conservative Refocus' take on all of this is that we do need to address those whom have coverage issues due to illness etc.; however, Obama's impetus does not offer any true solution. We have medical care already for the poor in the form of Medicaid. Medicare covers our seniors. The sub-section of mis-insured individuals in between are the ones that we should be focusing on; however, Obama and a preponderance of Democrats in Congress and the Senate propose to throw out the baby with the bathwater and remake our entire system for the benefit of a comparative minority. Why are we not surprised?

The Soft-Attack via Healthcare

Ownership of property by individuals was at the heart of The Framers efforts in establishing a system of Liberty for the individual rather than the State. To some Americans, this concept may seem alien since it is such a cornerstone of both our Nation and our economy in the present day. But over 200 years ago The Founders made this provision primary when initially framing our system because of the gravity-like magnitude that it conveyed in the form of individual rights. Now, the Government's efforts at invading—if not taking over control of the Healthcare Industry by way of its funding—is, in many ways, a foray into unconstitutionally seizing property that belongs to the Civil Society rather than the Government. The seeming reason for these constant attacks on the Healthcare Industry by Authoritarians is no accident. Heathcare Industry control by a single entity encompasses so many possible portals for invasion of individual rights that it is a constant target for true Statists. The Statist needs to control a single powerful sub-section before extending his reach into the individual's realm and grabbing control there.

How Did All of This Happen, Again?

A) The populace's dissatisfaction with the costly war effort led by a Republican President over these many years, coupled with a Democratic takeover of Congress in January 2007.

B) The loss of control by Conservatives on the spending purse strings, coupled with a Democratic push many years ago, as well as last year's government relaxation of safety nets in lending procedures.

C) Corporate "off balance book" transparent mortgage derivatives going bad as a result of declining mortgage performance, coupled with a lack of regulatory foresight.

D) Unprecedented over-purchase of bad mortgages by Fannie Mae and Freddie Mac which caused both entities to go in receivership and control by the Federal Government—all of which resulted in the 2008 meltdown.

E) The illusion that this was all Republican-based, which caused the populace to shift to the Democrats in subsequent elections.

F) The Mainstream Media's natural disdain for all things "not Liberal," refusing to properly vet candidates on their true positions.

Thus "A Perfect Storm"

There are many in our Civil Society whom have become despondent in these trying times for the attacks on our liberties that seem not to be rooted in any sort of paradigm that makes sense. The normal defenses that have customarily come to the aid of our free society have, in many ways, become absent. This is due in large part to the seeming complacency of many and their jaded view of politics as a whole, which must be coupled with the Mainstream Media's inability to report or not report events without any political bias. The events of the past five years, however, seem to have taught us a very hard but important lesson that none will soon forget. History is, at times, a cruel teacher.

Many have now learned what a smaller but more concentrated segment has always known. American Exceptionalism is not a myth. It is the culmination of thousands of years of tyranny at the hands of those whom would abuse their power over others as if it were a hobby to be enjoyed.

When Thomas Jefferson laid down the foundations of our government in concert with some of the most brilliant and capable men of theirs or any time, virtually every culture and historical system of government had been reviewed and debated in earnest before The Founders settled upon a Democratic Republic that could stand the test of time and tyranny. The rule of law, rather than of individuals or groups of individuals, had been determined to be the most enduring and foolproof of any system of government in theoretical existence. Thus was this nation born and then prospered to be the leader of all free men and an economic Eden that would become a beacon to all Peoples. There is a price for our fortune, however, and it involves an eternal vigilance that must be instilled within our progeny and maintained in earnest.

To those whom are fearful and despondent at what the future may bring, I will say this with great confidence:

Fear not.

This country has navigated far more difficulties too numerous to mention than this concentrated but ill-constructed attack by those whom feel certain that their oft-tried but ill-conceived way is the best way for all.

There are simply no people on this earth whom are more relentless, nor more courageous, than the individuals whom believe in the ideals that God created Man with certain inalienable rights—that among these are Life, Liberty and the Pursuit of Happiness.

We will peacefully persevere in regaining our governance in the way it was originally intended; however, now is the time for each of us that has true understanding of our Nation to begin if they have not done so already.

"For the sentiments of men are known not only by what they receive but by what they reject also."

~Thomas Jefferson

The Case for Capitalism: The Statist Menace

Week of 10/04/2009

Image 13

The President has—in yet another example of his disdain for victory with regard to anything beyond his personal ambitions—failed rather miserably in his attempt to gain the 2016 Olympics for his political and business "associates" in Chicago. The President had a truly compelling and original argument that those at the IOC had, no doubt, never heard before: "There is nothing I would like more than to step just a few blocks from my family's home with Michelle and our two girls and welcome the world back into our neighborhood" (The Huffington Post, 10/02/2009, "Obama's Olympic

Speech: 'I Urge You to Choose Chicago'").

One supposes this might be the Mother of all "Multi-Billion Dollar International *Emotional* Business Deal *Appeals*." The Mainstream Media reacted to the first round elimination of Chicago predictably—*that being hysterically.*

One particular CNN (Rubber Boat) Anchor blubbered in disbelief to such a degree that viewers, one must imagine, waited for him to let out a staccato, ululating wail of grief–then melt to the floor (after the cameras cut away) in a despaired and breathless effeminate faint of disbelief (and he was their *Iron Man*).

Can this "Messianic Misanthrope" actually accomplish anything that is TRULY good for his country, for Heaven's sake? Mr. President, one should point out that the Chief Executive's traditional homage to his "Domestic Town of Origin" (to replace birthplace) normally comes after the term in office has concluded and is typically in the form of a Presidential Library....not an Olympic Village ....Good Grief!

Capitalism under Attack (or Is It Just Halloween?)

The valid concern of virtually anyone (whose head is not firmly supplanted up his posterior) is that it would appear that Capitalism and our Free Market System have come under extreme attack since the advent of the newly elected Obama Administration and the unwieldy and democratically haphazard leadership of Speaker Pelosi and Harry Reid. The Senate, which has been described as the "cooling saucer" for the "hot teacup" that is the House, has been "barely functioning" in that the new Health Bill (OpenCongress.org, 10/2009, "S.1796-America's Healthy Future Act of 2009"), which was recently introduced by Max Baucus, has so many laughable (yet eerily spooky) provisions in it, that one might think it has been designed to commemorate the upcoming Halloween season. Reid recently also indicated that they would, yet again, try to brute-force the measure through in true "Texas Chainsaw Massacre" form (in keeping it seasonally thematic…oh and don't forget the Yes We Can campaign theme played backward…e*eeww…Goosebumps!)*

One thing the Legislative folk need to bear in mind in their upcoming healthcare deliberations this week: You will vote your conscience **and the People will then vote theirs**. THE PEOPLE can repeal what you pass (and you yourselves) within the elected post that you occupy. You have temporary power but THE PEOPLE have the ultimate power, and their memories will be as sound as Deep Blues.

Having said that, we all find this "*so really cool and exciting*" that our "New Government" cares so much for its Citizenry it's even merrily willing to scare the bejesus

69

out of "most" of us with these Free-Market /Liberty eviscerating provisions just to get us all in the mood for All-Hallows Day. What next? Haunted "ScarroWhite House" or "House and Senate Chamber of Horrors?" (Oh...wait...forget Christmas.....now we have Legislative Halloween all year!)

Granted it was indeed an early Christmas for the Democrats and their interwoven pet lobbyists with the "Stimulus Bill," and its Santa's Bag full of economically useless "shovel ready" projects. But what many did not realize was that the "shovel ready" referred more to what one might find on the floor of a stable rather than a true economic shock treatment for US industry.

This attack on Capitalism has come on the heels of what the Presidential Chief of Staff has referred to as "a crisis to be taken advantage of" (he was referring to the economic meltdown). Well, at least HE got something useful out of it—*one might suppose.* Former Fed Chairman Greenspan has also come out with a rather dour outlook on the US economy in 2010, while the Media has just reported that unemployment claims have gone up this past month of September. This is beginning to become a recurring theme under our Statist-controlled Government. The Statist portion of the Democrats seem to be operating under the underachieving premise that even if they actually accomplish something that is mildly good for the economy, the populace (still waiting) will look upon the "comparatively pathetic" feat as a crowning achievement in legislative jurisprudence. The truly "sarcasm inducing" explanation that they habitually tout being this Administration has increased jobs by 2-3 million (while actually losing 3-4 million jobs) is simply propagandistic hyperbole.

This particular rationale could only make logical sense to a brain-addled maniac; however, the White House Press Secretary has a way of explaining it that leaves everyone in the press room feeling all schmaltzy since they now understand it (for a few minutes at least). But then when the few inquiring minds that we have left in journalism start asking the tangential questions, the Administration's economic plausibility factor falls in on itself like a house of cards.

Why Is the Economy Continuing to Sputter?

With regard to this ongoing Capitalism Attack, one of the reasons this recession has been so long and so deep is due simply to the "imputed future" government philosophy of the current Congress and Administration to investors and business executives. Historically, the lows that we descend to (in our economy) during difficult times are followed by a corresponding high. However, in this case we seem to be sputtering along lethargically while being criticized for our overspending and anti-capitalist rhetoric/policy efforts from, amazingly, Socialist-Communist US Trading Countries, for Pete's sake! (And who can blame them?) The world economy is invested in the economic powerhouse that is the US. (As we go, so go they.) But does anyone not find it absurd that the world's shining example of "Free Market Economics" seems to be altering course into more of a regressive Socialist path?

This path of alteration has given virtually every business executive and investor in the US and abroad a severe case of the jitters—which translates into an economy that seems stuck in the mud. The drivers of the economy keep spinning the threadbare wheels in a vain effort to get the consarned thing out of the mud and moving again (the Chinese, by the way, are getting tired of pushing). But this is probably why the numbers coming out are so mixed. When the "economic vehicle" is stuck, one engages and disengages the wheels in a rocking effort. These mixed results coming out seem to equate quite aptly with the back and forth rocking effect. Were the Administration to actually utter something even vaguely promising to the business world, I expect our mud-marooned economy would quickly lurch back into motion.

All the while, both predominantly Democratic (branches) of our government and much of the "Celebrity Illuminati" have been decrying the terrible

illness that is Capitalism at every possible opportunity—
while hypocritically raking in cash and wealth at a
gleeful pace.

Cause de Célèbre

WE ALL KNOW what celebrities earn, while many, if
not most, decry the profits of corporate executives and
insurance companies—not to leave out energy
companies—while we all must choke down the costs of
theaters, concert tickets and over-priced music CDs and
videos, since it is purely a diversion and not truly needed
for quality of life. If this is, indeed, the case then why
does the government support and endow ventures such
as the National Endowment for the Arts and various
other "non-profit" organizations as numerous as the stars
in the nighttime North Carolina sky?

We are offered disparate arguments in this regard, but
can you just imagine the howls of protests from
Hollywood, the non-stop commercials and
Dixie "Chicken" regalements that we would have to
endure were the Government to reach into the
celebrities' pockets the way they have auto dealerships
and manufacturers and many other industries too
numerous to mention? We would not submit that the
entertainers' or athletes' salaries are too high, despite the
temptation, simply because as an avid Free
Market participant, I understand that one individual's *too*

high is another's *too low* and that it is all very subjective and relativistic to the point that only a Messiah could figure it all out and make it fair *(not!)*.

Michael Moore, who is valued at a net worth in excess of $50 million, would be the Chief Co-Conspirator of all the celebs—releasing a movie that decries and despises Capitalism as a scourge to the world while suckling from one of Capitalism's grandest teats, which would be akin to strangling the mother with one hand while consuming her nourishment with the other. Yet none of the imbeciles who will worship/view this movie will see the wretched hypocrisy of his actions (that we should celebrate such disingenuous fools).

Hypocrisy on Parade

But Nancy Pelosi—who never misses an opportunity to trash-talk any form of corporate profit or free enterprise--has an investment package of wealth that would turn even Warren Buffet's head. Her net worth has been estimated in the approximate range of $18.71 million, while Barack Obama, no net worth slouch, has wealth which is approaching $1.5-3 million (his book deal is a mystery). Harry Reid, whose rhetoric also falls on the anti-Capitalist side, is a millionaire several times over. These are the same folks who trash talk "exorbitant employee salaries" and wish to "spread the wealth" of we Americans (or at least what we have left) while stealthily imparting a Socialistic agenda that would force a sympathetic tear even from Karl Marx. They have their fortunes, I suppose, so screw everyone else!

I suggest we start with their wealth (Pelosi, Obama and Reid) and work our way down. Hey! If you're gonna talk the talk, ya' gotta walk the walk—leaders take the arrows and all. Has any cognitively activated Liberal (oxymoron?) out there even stopped and considered what truths have just been communicated and documented?

Conservative Refocus has endeavored to thoughtfully provide the facts—supporting details of our research below. I truly don't know which viral infection is worse, Progressive/Liberal Ostrichitus or the H1N1?

Barack Obama   Net Worth: $1.5-3 Million   2007
(Source One, Source Two)

Nancy Pelosi   Net Worth: $18.71 Million   2008
(Source Three)

Harry Reid   Net Worth: $1.5 Million   2003
(Source Four)

(Most likely, each of these figures is underestimated due to singular Congressional veracity.)

During all of this conflictive logic, the Media seems to plod along much like a blind and sickened Beast of

Burden that cares not to see what is actually going on and even less to report it since the "Emperor of All Ills" has taken his Arthurian throne. When did Free Market Capitalism (which is the engine along with our Individual Liberties that powered the United States into a Super-Economic Powerhouse) become an illness that needs to be corrected?

The recurring theme throughout man's recorded history, whether it be money-grubbing Televangelists, proselytizing Talk Show Hosts, or even trash-talking Politicians is that whatever the subject being lambasted and burned at the stake is, that
same persecuting individual or group of individuals is often simply trying to overcompensate for their own shortcomings or excesses by demonizing the very subject that they "secretly" hold so dear.

Source One: CNNMoney.com, 07/12/2007, "Millionaires-in-Chief: Obama's Money."

Source Two: Washingtontimes.com, 04/19/2009, "Exclusive: Obama's $500,000 book bonanza."

Source Three: rollcall.com, 09/22/2008, "The 50 Richest Members of Congress (2008)."

Source Four: CNN.com/Inside Politics, 08/13/2003, "Millionaires populate U.S. Senate."

The Dynamic Duo Rides Again: Rebutting Liberal Columnists in Defense of the Constitution

Week of 10/04/2010

Image 14

Here we go again.

I read with interest two Liberal Opinion articles that appeared within the Charlotte Observer ("The Politics of Spite" and "Dad's Life or Yours: Insurance Access Forces Choice") on October the 6th which were brimming over with Statist Dementia. *To be fair, I will remind all that the Observer edits a great deal (to save paper since pine trees are so scarce in NC?), so our links should be your source if you should wish to read the articles referenced here.

Apparently, The New York Times has dusted off their Liberal Heavyweights in Krugman and Kristof (sounds like a Barnum and Bailey circus act) and fired them yet again towards Rush Limbaugh (and anyone else on the Right) in addition to any sort of private industry (other than the Leftist Media) that is not in lock-step with their outdated and Titanically Left-Leaning agenda.

This dynamic duo has come out in a dual-pronged attack against anyone who dares question the President and anyone who dares question Universal (Imperialist) Healthcare.

Thou Shalt Not Criticize the President

Krugman, clearly smarting because those big, mean Constitutional bullies actually had the gall to laugh at the "Messianic Monolith" in his failed attempt to secure the Olympics for his home team of Chicago. Kristof, in his column, calls our Health Insurance System dysfunctional and drags out several truly unfortunate individuals—one who has—and then another who may have—a genetic disorder that imperils the continuance of their own respective insurance. The column then points up how things would be so much better if the Government were in charge so that this sort of thing would no longer happen. While at the same time today, a report was released that clearly indicates that one of the largest US government-run healthcare systems has a "denial of claims rate" that is twice that of ANY PRIVATE INSURER (American Medical Association, "2008 National Health Insurer Report Card"). So, Nick, where does one go when the Government says NO?

Then, Krugman states (under one of his many illusions) that "the modern Conservative movement dominates the Republican Party" and "has the emotional maturity of a bratty 13 year old." (This from the guy who still throws staplers at the wall in a rage because President Reagan got elected back in 1980.) He then goes on to call the celebration of America losing the Olympics "puerile," but never mind Krugman's "constant whining" about the War on Terrorism and the War in Iraq over the past number of years, while our brave and determined—and at this point demoralized—soldiers are making huge sacrifices in the interest of liberty (Politicalgas.org, 10/03/2009, "America's On-Going Crisis").

So let me see if I have this straight, it's "Bad-Bad Boys" to poke fun at the President's arrogance in what are ultimately just "games ," but THEN the war that can and does decide the safety and lives of Americans everywhere is free game and should be denigrated and lambasted at every opportunity (until it becomes the Democrats' responsibility)?

Just Tear It Down and Start Over—Government Is Always Better

Meanwhile, Kristof points up the legislation that is the "Genetic Information Nondiscrimination Act of 2008," that actually passed in order to correct this looming problem, and even states that it should eventually help this (admittedly valid problem), but then also states that insurance companies will still be able to discriminate against people who show symptoms...Huh?

Not according to Rep. Sue Myrick who just put forth a bill to finally close this vexing problem (house.gov, 10/07/2009, "Myrick Signs on to Alternate Health Care Plan") that they are likely to never pass. I will agree with Kristof that these problems should have been tackled some time ago (and have in some areas), but I find it interesting that rather than our Congress taking steps to close up these problematic issues long ago, they seem to have left the way open for their final solution. Our healthcare system has been lauded all over the planet as the absolute best in the world. The Statist Democrats—as represented by their actions of the past—would prefer to abolish the current system and remake it into something "better." This is akin to taking the largest and finest mansion on the planet (think Al Gore's home) and demolishing it simply because the plumbing leaks and the shingles are getting a little old, for Heaven's sake.

Semantically Harmful to the Cause

Back over to Krugman, who is now at the point where he acknowledges ideological differences within the parties, but then states the Republicans (laughably) have shown no consistency. Sorry there Paul, but the Republicans along with the American people, have been very consistent. Let's see, what was it? Oh! ...NO_NO_NO_NO_NO.

I must point out, that does seem invariably *consistent*, Sir, unless you view everything through the jaundiced eye of a Statist Liberal who believes that anything Private Enterprise can do would better done by the Government, despite all the mountains of evidence to the contrary. Then Krugman endeavors to sound like the authority on Medicare and states that the Republicans are basing their resistance on lies about death panels and such. Okay, I understand his argument. He wishes to call them "End of Life Counselors" and the Republicans wish to call them "Death Panels." I suppose this is just an issue of semantics, but I wonder if, like Congressman John Conyer, Mr. Krugman has actually read any of these Draconian bills? (Probably just taking the Democrats' word for it, yet again) Unless, of course, Big Brother is a Republican—then—Katie, bar the door!

But Where Will the Canadians Go Now?

Back over to Kristof, now—who actually has the unmitigated gall to call out members of Congress who oppose the plan (meaning Republicans) due to the fact that—get this—"they have first-rate healthcare [umm...it's a private plan, so no argument there] and so perhaps don't appreciate how their posturing forces people into impossible situations."

Ok, impossible situations? Do you mean like the one under Democrat Senator Max Baucus' initial plan that would force individuals to buy healthcare, and if they don't, they will pay a huge fine, and if they can't afford the fine they will be incarcerated? Now that is a truly impossible situation, Sir! But being the Authoritarian Apologist that he is, I can understand Kristof's precarious position.

Kristof then ends his column (thankfully) with a final comment that hopes that "the Legislators find it in their hearts to overhaul an existing insurance system that is the disgrace of the industrialized world." Yes sir, this is why a bunch of folks up in Canada are now vying for legislation that will allow them to outsource procedures (that cannot be done in time by the government- run system) to private providers within the US where there is no waiting period and, therefore, no immediate death sentence (latimes.com, 09/27/2009, "In Canada, a move towards a private health care option"). This is due to deathly waiting periods of up to 24 months and even longer (if ever) because of a shortage of the self-same necessary providers and—always—"the costs involved."

Krugman Still Argues with the Shadows of the Past

Back to Krugman, who now lambasts Newt Gingrich— reaching all the way, way back into the 1990's (can't you get any fresh material dude?) for trying to cut Medicare benefits while, ironically, the various Democratic bills in play plan to slash Medicare spending by 30%, not to mention the suspended COLA increases for our Seniors.

Then, laughably, he speaks to the President's plan to reduce Medicare expenditures when the only way to do that is to deny services and procedures or "ration" the care. He then, even more hilariously, describes the Republican Party ever since Reagan (yet again) of being full of apparatchiks—thanks! new word—and being dominated by Radicals and Ideologues that do not accept anyone else's right to govern. Mr. Krugman, Sir, in your world, Thomas Jefferson and every one of The Founders would be considered rabid Right-Wingers. I would point out only that there is a huge, gaping difference between Democratic governance and Fascism.

Hey! Let Go of My Club!

Finally, Krugman goes after Rush Limbaugh—one more time--and accuses him of suggesting that Hillary Clinton was a party to murder. Rush does tend to have a very sarcastic sense of humor that could be misinterpreted, but as a good friend of mine always says, "Sarcasm is what separates us from the other primates," so it does not surprise me that Krugman would throw that one out there.

Fascinatingly, one must again notice that Krugman seems to have a chip on his shoulder about events that happened long, long ago and have no real bearing on current events. In addition, I am rather cautiously concerned that Krugman might actually leap frog back all the way into the Republican Lincoln's day and vilify the Emancipation Proclamation while he's about it. At any rate, Krugman now accuses the Republicans of "seizing any club at hand with which to beat the current Administration," which—I must point out—is precisely what Krugman has been doing all of these years before the Statists took over. I know that Mr. Krugman has won a Nobel Prize for his "overflowing body" of Statist economic propaganda; however, I should point out that I, too, have a rather formidable cadre of awards.

Just to name a few, I was a proud recipient of a really cool basketball trophy when I was in the fourth grade (admittedly we only won 2 of 5 games), but in addition, I was awarded one of the highest honors that can be bestowed in North Carolina. I won a 10lb. frozen turkey in the Chadbourne, NC Local Turkey Shoot when I was in the 7th grade! Such was my popularity that I was able to trade the very tightly choked, but highly lauded, 4 by 10 gauge shotgun for a really snazzy 20 gauge double barrel. (Oh, and I won the NC Leadership Award in the year 2000—probably along with 770 others).

So take that, Mr. Nobel Prize Winning Liberal! Would you like fries with that, Sir?

Part Two: The Case for Capitalism: Attack of the Authoritarians

Week of 10/11/2009

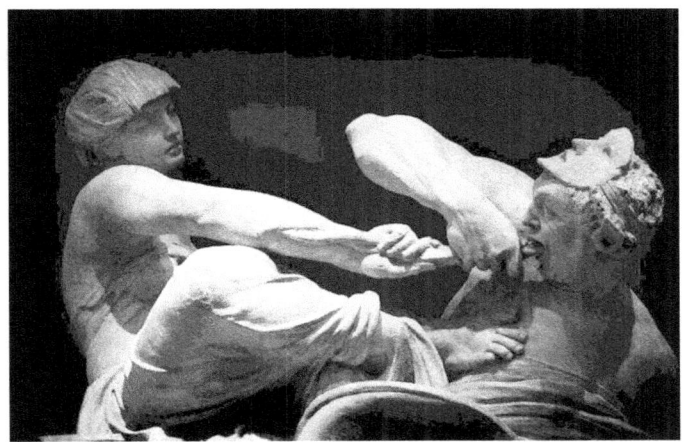

Image 15

As we all meander about in our lives within the crispness of autumn, we find that we are perpetually transfixed by the massive government focus on our healthcare system while our economy continues to tank. Many are still asking: "Why is healthcare almost exclusively at the center of the legislators' attention while we have more pressing problems to deal with?"

This both preceding, and also coming upon the heels of yet ANOTHER wondrous and awe-inspiring event where the President "magically" received a Nobel Peace

Prize based upon what he is "fixing-to-do," which is a "Nobel first" as far as we can tell.

My young son was all for this novel reward plan with regard to his grades, based upon the premise that he has every intent to make straight A's; therefore, they should be granted on this self-same basis.

At any rate, I wonder if perhaps this is a "giveback" by the Nordic Peoples for their failure to grant the Olympics to the President.

In addition to all of this, we now have the Senate dubiously approving the "idea of a bill" for the go-ahead to a new round of legislative healthcare meddling, rather than an "actual" bill.

October 31st Just Can't Come Fast Enough.....

The "Mad Scientist Senator," Harry Reid, in keeping with the legislative Halloween theme (please see, "The Case for Capitalism: The Statist Menace") has devised a nefarious scheme in which the current construct—having been accepted and which will go to committee—will be enjoined by the Houses' several miscreant healthcare ideas and then coupled to the TARP legislation—additional funding which will all be then voted upon. In other words, the current plan (America's Healthy Future Act of 2009) as devised will involve gathering a bunch of mismatched parts and pieces stealthily sewn together for the ultimate outcome, which will be Government-Controlled Healthcare, (i.e. the current legislative body's equivalent of a **Frankenstein's Monster**).

The jolt from the ensuing vote will then bring the Beast to life, and we shall all then quake at the power and wonderful ugliness of this artificial monster! All the while, there's Harry Reid—standing back, howling and cackling: "It's alive!! It's alive!!! In the name of Obama, We Have Done It!! It's alive!" (Note: Perhaps Reid needs to read the rest of the story. Just saying...)

Going back to this question of why healthcare is suddenly so important, the answer seems simple enough to anyone whom has studied the Constitution in an historical context. Once again, this is a power-grab by the Democratically- controlled Government that would be key in centralizing power and authority by the liberty-eviscerating Authoritarians, because "they know better than The Founders" (naturally).

The current healthcare system, for the most part, is privately owned and is, therefore, a "property" belonging to the Civil Society or Peoples of the United States. Private property rights are the keystone in a Democratic Republic, and this will be the first "major" incursion of (already) many into that domain. Once there, the ability to control lives by the government will be dramatically magnified in the interests of "cost savings" (among many others). A recent report from John Stossel outlined what the United States can expect, were She to adopt a healthcare plan predicated on the former and existing legislative attempts at passage of this bill.

Profit Is the Lubricating OIL of Any Venture and Any Healthy Economy

Waiting periods that are currently non-existent will become routine the longer the system is in place, along with the eventual shortage of facilities and physicians, which always accompanies this "Socialization" of medical care. Both the President's and the Democratic Legislators' rationale for this incursion seems to always fall back on attacking "profit." The Authoritarians define profit as something dirty, which, they think, should never enter into our healthcare system; however, the true definition is something any human being would recognize. Profit is defined as "the making of gain in business" and comes from the Latin word "to make progress." So, if we fall back on the true definition—and do a little sewing job of our own—it is apparent that the Democrats simply do not wish to make progress within healthcare--based on their actions—which negate the making of progress [or profit] in healthcare.

The Stossel report clearly shows why profit is such an important component within this venture. Speaking to profit as it applies to individuals, anything left over after we pay off all our bills is profit. We take vacations and go out to eat, etc.--on our own profit. (Liberal Democrats love profit only to the extent that it is.)

Profit speaks to improvement of lives.

In the healthcare business, profit speaks to finding new cures and new treatments, in addition to the wealth that sometimes comes with such ventures. The Authoritarians wish to remove this component from our healthcare. They blame their counterpart detractors as having "no plan." Well, I should point out that this whole charade of effecting legislation that will emasculate our current world-class Healthcare system deserves nothing but derision and rejection and should be laughed out of Washington at the first opportunity.

How Can We Fix the Existing Problems within Healthcare?

There are a number of problems which exist outside of the government's purview, simply because it has not yet endeavored to deal with those whom are making a decent income but cannot obtain insurance for various health reasons. There is already a model government insurance plan in place under Property and Casualty Insurance Coverage that could be emulated on the Health Insurance side as a government-funded (but still private insurance) outlet that could remedy this problem without costing $900 billion—in addition to raising health insurance and various other taxes and ruining the best system in the world. The **Government Flood Insurance Program** is that model.

By allowing the existing 1700 private health insurers (Yeah, that many! Bet lots of ya' didn't know that!) to underwrite the health plans based upon existing popular models (that could only be gotten by those whom have been turned down by traditional carriers) the government could remedy this problem while not breaking all of our banks. The individuals would still have to pay for their coverage, but the pricing would be based on existing rate-established models. This would involve extra cost to be funded by tax payers, but anything would be better than the Authoritarians' power-grab.

 Many of the people currently reading this column know exactly what I am referring to and can attest to the effectiveness of their flood insurance coverage— especially those in the Midwest. Many ask: Why does the government need to be involved in the issue of flood or healthcare insurance? Well, the answer when boiled down is this: "Adverse Selection."

This basically means that only the people whom actually need flood insurance will buy it. This adverse selection creates a rating disparity and would cause many private insurers to simply go out of business because a disproportionate number of folks with ailments/flood problems will always need the coverage. This same problem also would apply to health insurance. The premise of insurance coverage is always based on the spreading out of risks throughout as large a number of individuals as possible.

Doubtful Happenings and the Real Target

The above idea could be put into play quite easily with the help of our insurance carriers, whom wish to remain in business rather than being replaced by government bureaucrats (such greedy guys!). But is this going to happen? Doubtful, because this would endanger the seizure of additional power by those already IN power (though always ignorant of how these rules would be applied to them if they undergo an ejection from their post within their seemingly Socialist-Leaning Construct). They would have us drop a proven and beneficial system to all in order to take up a system that has been shown to fail time after time.

I believe Congressman Thaddeus McCotter (R-MI-11) said it best: "As a progressive party, Democrats will bring you change by using government to enhance revenues from the rich to invest in the production of energy and green collar jobs, and by using diplomacy to engage America's enemies and end the Iraq War."

Translation: "As a regressive party, Democrats will bring you the 1970s by using Socialism to raise taxes from you to waste in the production of lethargy and unemployment, and by using magic to appease America's enemies and lose the Iraq War."

As we can all see—the Democrats are doing a MARVELOUS job with the economy so far.

Since when did Free Market Capitalism, which is the engine— along with our Individual Liberties—that propelled the United States into a Super-Economic Powerhouse (the likes of which the world has never seen) become an illness that needs to be corrected, I ask once again? Socialism and Socialist-leaning policies have been gaining ground, most likely from within our liberal education system and from, apparently, too much luxury for some.

Define It and the Truth Shall Set You Free!

According to the World Heritage Dictionary, our form of government and economic system is not a virus in need of eradication nor is it a disease which one must continually live with in misery. (This may amaze some of you Liberals out there while you sip your lattes). Please see the below definitions to verify with your own eyes:

cap·i·tal·ism (kâp'ĭ-tl-ĭz'əm)

n. An economic system in which the means of production and distribution are privately or corporately owned and development is proportionate to the accumulation and reinvestment of profits gained in a free market.

Capitalism allows the free flow of market forces to supply needs to all consumers at all times and is a natural counterpart to a Democratic Republic in that any controls which are in place are there to regulate and mitigate excess rather than interfere in the natural order. Now let's look at Socialism:

So·cial·ism (sô'shə-lĭz'əm)

n. 1. Any of various theories or systems of social organization in which the means of producing and distributing goods is owned collectively or by a centralized government that often plans and controls the economy. 2.The stage in Marxist-Leninist theory intermediate between capitalism and communism, in which collective ownership of the economy under the dictatorship of the proletariat has not yet been successfully achieved.

Hmm…did you catch the second part of the Socialism definition? Socialism, according to The American Heritage Dictionary is, in essence, a means to Marxism.

While we are at it, since Socialism seems to lead to Marxism, let's just check out Marxism also:

Marx·ism (märk'sĭz'əm)

n. The political and economic philosophy of Karl Marx and Friedrich Engels in which the concept of class struggle plays a central role in understanding society's allegedly inevitable development from bourgeois oppression under capitalism to a socialist and ultimately classless society.

Class struggle? No, just money struggles for us all, right now!

Wonder, if out of each of these definitions, anyone may have noticed where the word "FREE" was deposited? Freedom is in no way associated with either Socialism or Marxism. I would be remiss if I did not throw in the most important definition: (I wonder if perhaps Marx or Engels had anything on Jefferson and Washington by way of either grey matter or character?) Now, our current form of government defined:

Re·pub·lic (rĭ-pŭb'lĭk)

n. 1. A political order whose head of state is not a monarch and in modern times is usually a president. A nation that has such a political order. A political order in which the supreme power lies in a body of

citizens who are entitled to vote for officers and representatives responsible to them. A nation that has such a political order.

2. A political order in which the supreme power lies in a body of citizens who are entitled to vote for officers and representatives responsible to them. A nation that has such a political order.

3. Often Republic, a specific republican government of a nation: the Fourth Republic of France, an autonomous or partially autonomous political and territorial unit belonging to a sovereign federation, a group of people working as equals in the same sphere or field: the republic of letters.

Here, one can see at a glance the differences between the three systems. I would ask: Which one of these would you prefer?

In 1787, as Benjamin Franklin was departing the historic convention that determined the course of the Nation, a woman asked him, "Do we have a monarchy or a democracy?" He replied, "A Republic, if you can keep it." Prophetic words, those.

The Authoritarians Dual Attack on Form of Government and Form of Economic System

The assaults on our form of government in the shape of bank takeovers, student loan programs, mortgage lending, two of the top three US based vehicle manufacturers, and now the effort at government-run healthcare (among a host of many other items) should leave only the grandest of imbecilic idiots to wonder if their freedoms are being endangered. In our history, these events are unprecedented. It is also a fact that virtually every fascist, dictator, emperor and what not were Left-Leaning Authoritarians or, in other words, Democrats on steroids (think Barney Frank as the Incredible Hulk and you will be on the right path to understanding my point). No Right-Leaning Republican has ever grabbed for Authoritarian power because the Repubs are "individual rights junkies."

Normally, within a political period, issues are brought forth and corrected—sometimes big, sometimes small. But in this case, never have we had so many political issues over so many ranges brought forth and thrust into votes where the American people would be sorely, if not harmfully affected and forced to endure changes that they neither need nor want. This is how one can tell that the normal government of the past has been starkly altered into something invasive and overbearing– something that does not allow change to occur through means that are positive but rather by forcing the changes upon the people. If change is attained in this manner it is not for the sake of Democracy but rather something…else.

We have seen American flags being altered with Obama's image, we have the President indirectly involved in a name-list for dissenters, we have the Prez involved in actuating change through his office and in support of his programs; we have a Prez that disavows funding of ACORN during and after making them a huge part of his campaign; we have a Prez that gets the final votes on a Nobel 14 days after entering office—he was barely in the White House, for Heaven's sake...on and on and on. All of this seems to be in the interest of furthering the President's now-waning popularity.

We Can Beat 'Em with One Arm Tied Behind Our Backs (Uh...Maybe?)

In addition to all of this, we have a Commander in Chief who seems to be sorely at odds with his Generals in the Afghanistan Campaign to wipe out Terrorist strongholds. The problem being, to use an apt analogy, the Prez seems to want to conduct the war with a force that is inadequate to the task. Since war is a contest decided by two teams or opposing forces, we can draw an analogy for the President that he should easily be able to identify with—since he's a big sports fan.

Take basketball or even football for instance—or any team sport. In the big play, most often the other team will always score when a defender is out of place or has been mis-assigned or there are too few men on the field. Further, this type of mistake is one which the opposing team will nearly always capitalize upon (it ain't rocket science). This often happens due to poor coaching (hint-hint) or poor preparation; however, in this case, we have a president whom is publicly agonizing over making a decision which finally proved historically instrumental approximately 18 months ago—that decision being: The troop surge in Iraq which decided the victory of Iraq over its insurgency problem.

If the President does not wish to utilize a large portion of the forces which should be and are departing Iraq and get a sufficient number into Afghanistan, then he should simply pull all of our men off the field before they are overcome and decimated by the enemy. We, the American People, will then be able to aid our brave troops by fighting alongside them on our Homeground where the enemy will most likely end up, once again— and make no mistake, he will try at some point.
You may scoff at that—perhaps—but had any one of us ever assumed that we would be attacked by our own fleet of civilian aircraft as on 9/11?

One should finally take note—enumerable powers being granted to the government can be likened to a Beast whose growth knows no limitation beyond what it is being fed. The more sustenance the creature is given, the larger and more demanding of such morsels the Beast becomes. Before long, the Beast desires to take his own food rather than wait for the generosity of his master in that he will now become the master and the former master becomes the supplicant. This is the form of government that the Authoritarian or Statist Democrats seem to find most appealing.

And Atlas shrugged......

The Fourth Estate: The Administration Broadsides Fox News and the Constitution

Week of 10/18/2009

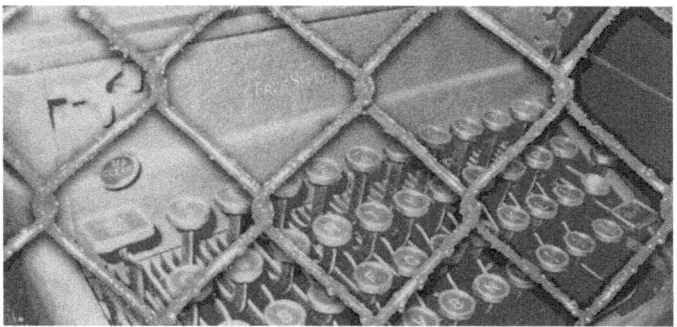

Image 16

This week we have had the distinct displeasure of hearing the President come out and attack yet another US Industry—this one being those dastardly "Vampirish" Health Insurance Carriers (no surprise there). Why? He claimed that they "used smoke and mirrors" in that they have the unmitigated gall to actually defend themselves from the repeated attacks of our government, and in actuality, who can blame them? However, attacking insurance companies was just the beginning. (I wonder if smoke and mirrors were commonly used before teleprompters with regard to the President's expert use of both?)

Mao Say Who?

The President's staff came out in a full phalanx attack against the only one true remaining member of the Fourth Estate—**Fox News**—for "reporting the news with a certain perspective." That perspective being one that differs from the President's, which is, apparently unacceptable, one might suppose. It is indeed unfortunate that the President and his staff fail to place such diligent efforts on the war in Afghanistan or the malaise in the economy.

Also in the news, we have Presidential Staffer, Anita Dunn, announcing in a graduation ceremony that Mao Tse Tung was one of her favorite political philosophers. In addition, we have Ron Bloom, who is the "Manufacturing Czar," indicating that he agreed with Mao that "political power comes largely from the barrel of a gun." The former Premier of China being a mass murderer of more than anywhere from 34 million to 71 million people whom dissented with him. Here at Conservative Refocus, we truly hope that this is not the future desire and imperative of these particular staffers; I can only speak for myself in particular.

The fact that the Prez has elected to surround himself with questionable ideologues from the extreme Left should apparently give us no pause, though we have evidence of relationships that stream back beyond 20 years (conservativerefocus.com, 10/20/2009, "Obama's Marxist Connections"), which, in fact, seem to represent the principles of Marxist Russia rather than the US. The Mainstream Media, that being nearly any outlet other than Fox News, chose not to vet these individuals within the President's past—this despite their job, as members of the Fourth Estate, to report objectively any matter which weighs in on a certain newsworthy political event no matter what that event might be. We are then summarily tasked (by our feckless leaders) as discerning members of society, to blink and wave off the obvious disparity between our sentiments and those of radical left-wingers.

I Will Fight for the President's Rights…but Will He Mine?

Please, don't get me wrong. This is, in truth, America, and I will fight for the President's right to have an extreme viewpoint despite the fact that it flies in the face of my beliefs. But the problem I see here is simply that neither the Press nor the President could, in actuality, be truthful about the views that Obama held in abeyance until such time as his position had been fully realized. The President's stance on any Capitalist tradition has been one of disdain at best. He has played to the Unions and the members of Chicago's Politico favorably; however, I have yet to see or hear him come out in praise and defense of the Constitution or any other mainstream

AMERICAN tradition or set of beliefs—beyond the Trade Unions.

With the President's repeated attack on virtually every major US industry—but now the Press itself, also—we must note a most disturbing trend unprecedented in Presidential history taking place. This is, indeed, the most *unpresidential President* we have ever had.

The unassailable fact is that the President took an oath to support and defend the Constitution of the United States when he accepted his office. The Constitution's First Amendment states unambiguously that the Press shall have unencumbered freedom to report as it sees fit. By attacking Fox News, the President has now imperiled the First Amendment that he swore to uphold. The other members of the "sycophantic Axis Press" continue to carry the Administration's water, no doubt in a cloud of cowardice which must be nothing more nor less than "fear" of upsetting the "Messianic Magi," in addition to their obvious approval of him with regard to their lack of true vetting during the campaign—which is the principle job of the Fourth Estate.

Ok...Cowards or Racists ...Please Make up Your Minds

Actually, the fact is that, due to the artful architecture built within our system, the Prez has no more nor less rights than me or you or even perhaps the beloved illegal aliens that the Democrats seem to coddle at every opportunity—despite their being ILLEGAL. Now, some might see that last remark as an attack on Hispanics when in fact it is a simple statement of truth with regard to the law of the land. If a disproportionate sector of the populace finds a particular statement to be injurious to their current position then shall those of us who make the observations be harangued for enabling their culpability? Or is it the old "Kill the Messenger" fall-back position?

We also have race being brought to the forefront of the news due to Rush Limbaugh's ejection from his bid to be an owner in the NFL. Attorney General Eric Holder, back in early 2009, described Americans as being "cowards" when it comes to discussing issues of race. However, when any White person attempts to address race in an honest way within the Media, he is both assailed and reviled and then automatically referred to as a racist.

Now, that being not enough, we also have Juan Williams, a Black Democrat who is a Contributor with Fox News, and who I greatly respect despite political differences, being told to "go back to the porch" by Black Radio Jock, Warren Ballentine, who disagreed with Williams as it concerns the racist label being applied to Limbaugh. Williams was defending a particular position of Limbaugh's. I actually felt bad for

Williams due to the fact that—as a Black Commentator—if he is forced to take a view with respect to his conscience that most other Blacks might find disagreeable to their own "cultural view," then he is denigrated and despised for thinking outside of what is admittedly the self-damaging maelstrom of current Black culture.

Hormonal Racist Paperclips

The simple fact is that by the current party's Demagogic and tireless use of the words *racist* and *racism* as being applied to anyone whom disagrees with the President (on the purported basis that he is Black) is, in essence, diluting the impact of the word to the point of inanity. The word will soon take on the gravity of a **paperclip** in its constant misusage as a tool by the extreme Left to discredit those whom disagree within the political process. Indeed, we are not surprised. It has been our experience in viewing the typical political stance of most Liberals as being simplistic and easily defeated by common sense without even a semblance of knowledgeable political "back support." Common sense is, however, not enough when dealing with the haphazard emotional histrionics of most Liberals when defeated by their own faulty logic.

We have seen what happens when an industry embraces the current government's direction of attack. When Bank of America, one of the most recent beneficiaries of the government's unending gratitude, was strong-armed (during the financial meltdown) to complete its purchase of an ailing Merrill Lynch, the government then—after the fact—burned the bank at the stake for contractually living up to Merrill Lynch's Employee Bonus Programs in a classic damned-if-you do-damned-if -you-don't scenario.

The simple fact is, the bank had no choice--but that's beside the point, I suppose. Contracts be damned! Merrill's employees did not deserve the bonuses according to the government, so that's it. One has to wonder if the outcome would have been different had the previous administration been in charge (still). As a result of all this, the Chairman of the Bank, Ken Lewis, recently resigned and then had his yearly pay unceremoniously cancelled—adding insult to injury, no doubt.

Of Clowns and Donkeys and Bears...Oh My!

The Government has, in addition, cancelled a large portion of dealerships for both Chrysler and GM on the basis that there were too many dealerships. Um... excuse us, but getting supply to customers is, easily, one of the basic foundations of marketing and product delivery. The Administration, in an apparent miasma of Capitalist confusion, was under the distinct misimpression that too many dealerships would drive down the price of cars? Hate to break it to you clowns, but we also have foreign dealerships as plentiful as fire ant hills in and about most areas of the US, so guess what Brainiacs?

This is our new government in full "Capitalist Kicking" mode. The signal that this sends to US Industry and Business promises to keep the Stock Market in a semblance of shock for some time to come—ergo—the recent disposition of virtually every economic indicator and analyst that we are living in a Bear Economy (or should that be bare?) which will continue for some time to come.

When next you open your 401-k statement or your Social Security check or even your unemployment check, why not then contact your local Congressperson and Senator and ask them what it is that they are doing to help you? The highly touted Stimulus IS NOT WORKING. The Stimulus needs to be repealed and a true second Stimulus in the form of temporary tax relaxations across the board—including a temporary cessation of FICA—will easily catch this economy on fire and into surge mode. Will they do it? Doubtful (yet again). The Liberals are nothing if not predictable and require mountains of pork for their pet projects—the populace be damned.

The largesse of Corporate America and Small Business and individuals is what supplies jobs and government funds as a result of fair taxation. It is certainly not the Treasury of the government. Now, if we can just get Obama and the Democrats in the legislature to understand this before it's too late....but would it, in truth, matter to them?

"Experience has shown that even under the best forms of Government, those entrusted with power have over time and by slow operations, perverted it into Tyranny"

~Thomas Jefferson

Mainstream Media's Mythos: How Well Does U.S. Healthcare Quality Actually Compare?

Week of 10/25/2009

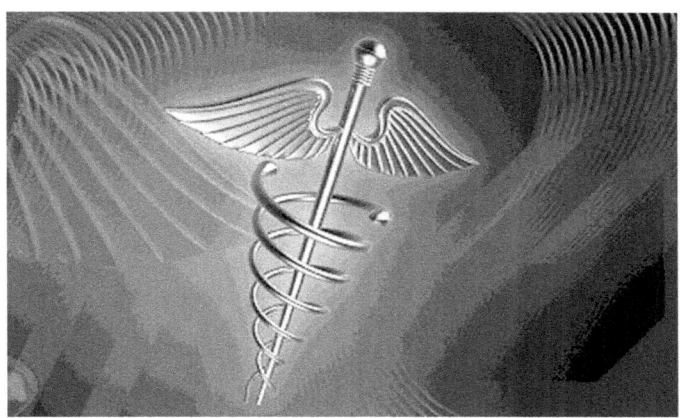

Image 17

With regard to the ongoing contentious battle over healthcare and the efforts by the opposing political factions to either illegitimately control it or to allow the remaining non-social (natural marketplace forces) to determine the authentic direction of medicine's flow—we thought it might prove interesting to look at a number of facts that seem to be missing in the debate.

On its own, the debut Conservative Refocus article "Mainstream Media's Holographic Reality" has generated a readership of nearly staggering proportions. We have been amazed—not only by the interest generated but also by what the information covered in the article implies (which is in direct contradiction to both our Fearless Leaders in the Government and our Media—such as it is).

The initial report, as detailed below, shows how far ahead the US is with regard to Healthcare Quality in comparison to any other population of similar size:

Comparison in Healthcare Quality of the Top (5) Most Populated Countries

Quality Rank	Country	Population	Life Expectancy	Total Population Rank
#1	The United States	303,825,000	78.2	#3
#2	China	1,330,040,000	73.18	#1
#3	Brazil	196,343,000	72.4	#5
#4	Indonesia	237,512,000	70.7	#4
#5	India	1,148,000,000	64.7	#2

Comparison Inserts:

Country	Population	Life Expectancy
European Union	499,794,855	77.32
United Kingdom	51,100,000	79.4

**Date sources: CIA Factbook 2009; 2009 United Nations Healthcare Census

Somewhat surprising, wouldn't you say? So it's not as bad as one might have been led to believe by both the Government and the Mainstream Media; in fact, it is quite the opposite. (For our complete analysis, please refer to "Mainstream Media's Holographic Reality.")

In addition to the facts we initially covered, there are a few other interesting data comparisons that the Socialist Eggheads just seem to "simply overlook"—most likely due to the fact that the truth tends to massively foul-up their arguments in support of government-controlled healthcare.

The first element of our comparison should, of course, initially setup the scale in which we are observing all of the data. So let's look at what our total respective **Healthcare Comparison Economies** produce while we are all "still" Capitalists:

Country—Selected for Medical System Comparison	Gross Domestic Product (in Millions)
United States	$14,204,322
China	$4,326,187
United Kingdom	$2,645,593
Brazil	$1,612,539
Russian Federation	$1,607,816
Canada	$1,400,001
India	$1,217,490
Indonesia	$514,389

Wow! Did you notice? It's enough to make even the most ardent Capitalist blush with regard to those stunning comparative numbers. But those US numbers appear to be dropping fast—just to be fair and to make all the Socialists and Left-wingers feel better. (Gee...wonder why?)

Ok, so I know what you're wondering, and here is the answer to your naturally competitive/inquisitive mind **outside** of the medical system comparison:

Top Ten Countries—GDP	Gross Domestic Product (in Millions)
United States	$14,204,322
Eurozone	$13,565,479
Japan	$4,909,272
China	$4,326,187
Germany	$3,652,824
France	$2,853,062
United Kingdom	$2,645,593
Italy	$2,293,008

Wow, again! When the Government and the Media keep insisting on how horrible our country is and how we squander the world's resources, they invariably seem to leave out just how productive "We the People"—living in our Free Market Economy—are and that we are producing a better-than-substantial proportion of the world's economy.

Now, since that's been settled, let's look at how much we spend per person on our healthcare coverage, as well as our per capita income:

Country—Ordered by Ranking of Income per Capita	Income per Capita—Using PPP Method	Per Capita Expenditures on Healthcare—US $	Expenditures, Private—Percentage of GDP	Socialized Healthcare—Yes or No
United States (#3)	$37,500	$6,096.2	8.52%	No
Canada (#11)	$29,740	$3,037.6	2.96%	Yes
United Kingdom (#21)	$27,650	$2,899.7	1.11%	Yes
Russian Federation (#82)	$8,920	$244.7	2.32%	Yes
Brazil (#86)	$7,480	$289.5	4.04%	Yes
China (#118)	$4,990	$70.51	2.91%	Yes
Indonesia (#141)	$3,210	$32.5	1.84%	Yes
India (#143)	$2,880	$31.4	4.14%	Yes

It would seem that—with higher life expectancies and world best-of-class healthcare—an individual's costs within the higher paradigm of per capita income should logically be a bit higher since the individual is in control of their own healthcare. In addition, our system pays what could be considered a very comfortable living to some of the best and the brightest in the world and by doing so attracts a great many doctors from all over the planet. This can be attested to by the number of foreign doctors who have migrated to the US in order to seek a higher income and better lives. You know, the fabulous doctors that we all run into in our daily lives who are still a bit sketchy on their command of the English language. I expect—with the rationing which is involved with any government health plan—the number and quality of our doctors would most likely decline over time; this would also incur the byproduct of "waiting periods" for necessary but non-emergency care.

Now, let's look at total number of all Physicians and Healthcare Providers including Dentistry—a valid inclusion (I should point out that dental speaks to overall healthcare quality far more than the Eggheads might suggest—ask any Cardiologist):

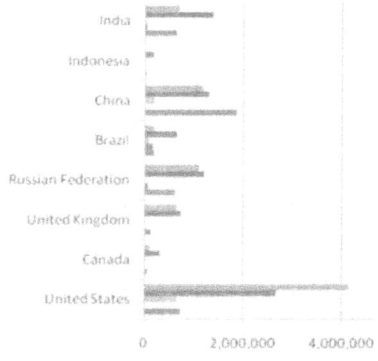

Legend:
- Number of Other Healthcare Providers
- Number of Nursing and Midwifery Personnel
- Number of Laboratory Health Workers
- Number of Environmental and Public Health Workers
- Number of Physicians

Now these are simply staggering numbers when you consider that we are comparing our many and varied available facilities and personnel to countries that have populations easily three or even four times the size of our population. This particular comparison simply begs the question: Why does a competitive marketplace medical system absolutely dwarf socialized medical countries with regard to the available number of facilities and personnel? Once again: Government care must naturally involve rationing in order to control costs.

Next we look at the number of hospital beds per capita, because this speaks to patient availability within a given country:

Country	Hospital Beds per 1,000 People	Socialized Healthcare—Yes or No
United States	3.3	No
Canada	3.7	Yes
United Kingdom	4.2	Yes
Russian Federation	10.5	Yes
Brazil	2.7	Yes
China	2.45	Yes
Indonesia	6	Yes
India	0.9	Yes

There is one particular wildcard when considering the number of hospital beds, and it is in regard to Outpatient Surgery Centers. The fact is simply that the US has progressed so far within the medical arts that doctors **here** can perform far fewer invasive surgical procedures, thereby far lessening the negative effects on patients. Now a particular procedure in the US can be completed and the patient sent on their way in three hours—which when done ten years ago might have required a three-day bed stay. Thus this would equate a need for far fewer hospital beds.

Outpatient Centers currently number approximately 5,000 spread throughout the US and are rapidly increasing as a measure to control costs as well as to serve patients more readily. This type of center was started in the US back in the 1970's and is now catching on in other countries. With Free Market principles in place, new types of treatments in the art of medicine continue to rapidly increase. But with socialized medicine, we can say goodbye to rapid innovations—which are initially too costly and offer no profit incentive.

Finally, as we all can see, the US is like an oasis within a desert when compared to other countries that have socialized medicine. Our quick study did not even look into the sterling cleanliness of most US facilities, nor did it look at treatment mortality rates—perhaps fodder for another in-depth look at the US medical system in comparison to others.

The Final Budgetary Solution (until that's gone, too)?

One final point that I find interesting, if not perplexing, is the ratio differences when we compare the Canadian system with the US system. Many have asked the question (including me) why are the Liberal Democrats and President so insistent on taking over the system, aside from the obvious answers indicated in my previous work? If one notices the total per capita income of the

US as opposed to the total per capita income of Canada—and then subtracts the amount that we spend on OUR medical treatments—we find that the per capita income becomes nearly equal. Then, when we look at the total amount the Canadian government spends on its citizens' medical care, which is about half of what Americans spend, the possible answer to this question becomes clearer.

The total Canadian expenditure for healthcare is approximately $3,000 per capita per year, as opposed to the United States, which spends approximately $6,000 per capita per year. When one looks at the US' entire budgetary income for 2009 the total is $2.1 Trillion. While the latest figures available show the total expenditure in the US for healthcare is approximately $2.3 Trillion per year. **If the US Government could hypothetically gain control over healthcare and then essentially halve the amount that it pays on healthcare—as in Canada—the government then could have an extra $1 Trillion to put towards wealth redistribution and/or whatever else it desires, including shortfalls.** This would assume that we would all be paying into the government essentially what we pay into our entire healthcare system (and the like) currently.

In Benjamin Franklin's day, as the Minister Plenipotentiary for the American Revolutionary

Government, Franklin's chief job was to facilitate diplomacy with regard to the French, but in particular his focus was the procuring of loans from the French government in order to finance America's war effort against the British. A fact that is often lost in the history books is simply that—without the French's help—our independence may have never actually happened. Historically speaking, D-Day, then, was in essence figurative payback.

Must Be Something in the Water Up There....

The problem—in our current context—was simply as follows: Even in Franklin's day, the Continental Congress of the existing body of states was so ravenous in its incessant spending that Franklin actually became embarrassed at his having to beg the French for more war funds on behalf of his country on a wearily continuous basis. If not for his singular celebrity-like popularity with the French peoples, he might not have been able to obtain the funds at all.

On this basis, one must suppose, whatever is in the water of the Potomac has most obviously been there for at least 250 years, for Heaven's sake.

Always follow the money...especially when Congress is involved. We are all aware of the studies that have come out indicating that the US pays far too much for its healthcare.

Has anyone considered the possibility that perhaps all the other socialized medicine countries are paying too little?

A Glorious Cause: The Return of the True Conservative

Week of 11/01/2009

Image 18

As the Liberals, who have been in charge of our government, drunkenly guzzle down the last few remaining drops of their debauched and radical "Statist binge," I suppose we all now get to see who eats the worm.

The Mainstream Media's disavowal of our "Non-Event" Tea Parties appears to have been "slightly off" in their faulty (as usual) analysis.

The predicted backlash against the extreme Left-Leaning Anti-Free Market policies of the current Administration and the Legislature is making itself starkly manifest within the latest round of elections. In addition, we have seen the sole remaining "Independent" American auto manufacturer, Ford Motor Company declare a profit this last quarter of nearly $1 Billion dollars. On the one hand, we have Big Government in command and control in true Fascist form (hey! Look the word up!) of two of the big three auto makers, and on the other hand, we have Ford Motor Company still in control of its own Free Market destiny. Now, I need not point out which one of these, with regard to "The Case for Capitalism," is sizzling along. The Democrats, not surprisingly, seem dejected as a result—offering various tepid excuses as to why Government is failing and Private Industry is surpassing with regard to Obama's "Union giveaways" of GM and Chrysler (which continue to struggle under "The Motor City Messiah's" iron-fisted leadership).

Purple Rino Secret Agents?

This week we have also seen a true Conservative candidate's moral triumph over a "Republican in Name Only" or "Rino" after the race became heavily publicized as a result of former Senator Fred Thompson and his politically astute wife Jeri Thompson—who had reported the events to Sean Hannity. The Conservative Media, and later (of course) the Mainstream Media, then began focusing attention on the New York 23rd District race.

Rush Limbaugh, who is inarguably the most prolific Conservative Analyst/Newsfeed out there, in concert with Fox Network icons Hannity and Glenn Beck, then repeatedly weighed in on the facts surrounding Independent Doug Hoffman (who is the actual Conservative Republican candidate) who then figuratively took Dede Scozzafava to the woodshed—this despite Scozzafava's rather clueless backing by other heavyweight Conservative well-knowns (Bloomberg.com, 11/02/2009, "Republican Scozzafava Backs Democrat in New York Congress Race").

Scozzafava is certainly entitled to her beliefs and positions as well as which party she identifies with, one must argue. However, the "automatic Conservative pass" that candidates have been afforded by (say-so) in previous contests has most likely come to an end. The core Conservative values that have been co-opted out of the Conservative identity are, many believe, what has actually led to the seeming confusion within the electoral recognition of Republicans. Not to mention the lack of "objectively disinterested" vetting that our Media now leaves up to local political Bloggers—unless the subject runs counter to Big Media's wishes. Nevertheless, Republicans have been automatically assumed to be Conservatives despite all of the evidence to the contrary with regard to events of the past several years. This might partially explain the heavy pummeling we Conservatives have taken in the election results of the last few cycles.

Scozzafava later, in an apparent "feces sling" at her Conservative supporters, promptly endorsed the Democratic candidate running against Hoffman after she found herself a distant third in the polls and then dropped out of the running. After a tight race, Hoffman predictably lost to the Democrat Bill Owens since the actual Republican vote was—at this point—hopelessly confused (to be nice). There have been reports that Obama—in the latter part of these events—weighed into the mix and "ingratiated" an endorsement from Scozzafava in favor of the opposition Liberal candidate (The Spy Who Came in from the Cold...perhaps?)

Statist Gymnastics and Dante's Inferno

In the Governor's race in Virginia, the true Conservative, Bob McDowell, also has won against his Democratic opposition despite the "Messianic Rainmaker's" insistent support of Creigh Deeds—who seemed to be scrambling away from Obama's endorsement as fast as he could (unfortunately for Deeds, the Prez was faster). The entire Virginia ticket was dominatingly won by Conservatives from the top down. New Jersey's Governor's race was also (amazingly) won by the Conservative there, Chris Christie; in addition, there were plenteous Conservative victories speckled profusely all throughout the political landscape as well.

Thus the Return of the True Conservative begins.

The Democrats, as with their opposites, always willing to parlay current elective victory into future abysmal defeat, have seen fit to install a seemingly anti-Constitutional and "radical" left-wing triumvirate of President and House Speaker and Senate Majority Leader. The Unholy Trinity of these three has essentially used the Constitution as a trampoline, damnably bouncing up and down on the thing as if trying to sunder the cloth of the venerated and celebrated document in a seeming attempt to bring the entire assembly crashing down on itself.

As a result of a little-talked-of ideological schism within the Democratic Party, the more Statesmen-like Democrats, or "Blue Dogs," have now found themselves heavily exposed, as if caught in a Liberal blizzard without any visible means of staying warm enough to survive. They can figuratively shake hands with the Devil, join up and thereby remove themselves from the harsh Democratic campaign defunding (the left-wing leaders are threatening), or they can huddle up together in the frigid party "exterior landscape," thereby avoiding the "hellishly hot and miserable Trio's anti-Constitutional pathos" in its radical demeanor, which only promises more of the same but the campaign funds will be there—less the votes of course (eenie-meenie-minie mo anyone?).

I think I might personally prefer to remain in the harsh exterior climate, gather lots of firewood and wait for the "Liberal Storm" to pass were I one of many of these "Ideological Democratic Party Orphans." (So how did you guys end up voting on your leadership again?)

Blizzards, Brevity, Trees & Bushes

Image 19

The blizzard indicated above, however, was not limited to the elements. A Paperwork Blizzard has meanwhile been artificially induced by our Democratic Congress in its ongoing battle against "pulp trees" when Pelosi came up with, yet again, a new House bill that was no less than 1,900 pages long. Then Harry "The Lumberjack" Reid, not to be outdone, produced a three-foot-high, 2,400-plus page Healthscare Bill (straight from Halloween to

Christmas, eh Mr. Reid?). The only things missing are the bulbs and the twinkling lights (and we took care of that).

Incidentally, there are, on average, around 1,300 pages in the King James Version of the Christian Holy Bible (just saying...). If indeed brevity is the soul of wit then the budget is not the only area where the Democrats are consistently deficient.

One can just imagine Greenpeace attacking our Legislative body for its obvious war on trees. Apparently this massive paper churning effort might be a part of the Stimulus plan. Our Legislature, in its seeming attempt to protect the paper companies, has taken the bull by the horns and is single-handedly stimulating the paper producing industry by virtue of the constant downpour of new, if not ill-fitting, bills coming out which must then be distributed to each member (so that they can then **not** read it).

I should point out only that Obama will be very grumpy if he finds his White House Christmas tree delivered in the form of a massive cone of confetti since all of the other American paper trees have been shredded and pulped by Congress. However, President Bush will most likely be blamed for this—also—on the strong evidence that he dislikes trees, since he is a Republican and is, most obviously, indeed a Bush...alas.

Media Finally Loses Fascination with Navel?

The Mainstream Media, meanwhile continues in its state of semi-denial as indicated in an earlier article ("A Natural Intensity Unfolding: We the People, Politics, and the Press"), but did pull together somewhat when confronted by the Administration's attempts to stifle the First Amendment and oust Fox News from impending press conferences. The New York Times, which most Conservatives love to hate (including this one) due to its extreme Left-Leaning agenda, pulled a surprise rabbit from its hat and stepped into the fray blocking the White House's attempt at censure of Fox News.

Now, perhaps this was a self-interested move, but most of us Conservatives could only respond in wide-eyed, jaw-dropping wonder and confusion at this spectacle. Can anyone actually imagine what might have happened had former President Bush tried to block and censure The New York Times?

The interesting part of all of this is that the Liberal Democrats, after installing changes within the system designed to make their policy leadership easier, have forgotten the one true constant within our American system: Whatever the one dominating party instills within its time of leadership becomes the replacing party's advantage. This is not to mention the old axiom which states that "revenge is a dish best served cold." In this particular case, after having been constantly denied true input within these Democratic policy remake decisions, the Republicans have a freezer the size of the Arctic that they would like the Democrats to explore, and I expect that they have selected an appropriate expeditionary tour guide in the form of Republican Senator Olympia Snow (she should blend right in with the Democrats—as usual).

The Case for Capitalism and the Republic

Within this Three Part Series in "The Case for Capitalism," we have taken a good look at our Capitalist system and how it's being threatened by those who think they know better. We have in Part One pointed out the extreme hypocrisy on exhibit by the Statist Liberals in their love-hate relationship with profit and their veiled threat against the Constitution. In Part Two, we looked at the various government systems and how they compare in concert with the heated attacks on our liberties in the form of a forced passage of the Healthcare Bill, among other incursions. In this, Part Three, we have seen the response of the American People in the form of reasserting their Conservatism— although we have much further to go. I must point out that the election results of this week, in concert with, this, our Return of the Conservative title, was no accident in its playful and yet apt allusion to a very popular movie series. You see—I have a great and boldly enduring faith in both the will and the wisdom of the American People.

Many people come to me and they say, "Hey—are those Liberal Democrats up there insane? Are they trying to get booted out of office? Do they actually despise normal Americans?" It genuinely seems that way at times, but in retrospect, I have often thought that the Liberals are, in actuality, the "OCDs" of the political world.

Obsessive Compulsive Disorder is for the most part a harmless condition in which the "victim" is constantly trying to keep complete order of all the myriad and varied items within their immediate environment. I suppose we all have a touch of this, but there are more extreme cases—you know the ones, they sit down at a table in order to dine and you cannot help but notice them constantly striving to keep every knife and fork on the table—along with the napkins, bowls, etc., in perfect alignment and order down to the tassels on the place settings—in some extreme cases.

I will often find myself while in the presence of such a person, disheveling things on purpose just to watch in secret amusement how they respond. In some instances, it seems almost a relief for them to find something not in perfect alignment with its "fellows" in a given setting, and then be able to correct the item. This seems to give them a sense of great satisfaction at having been able to place "the universe" back into strict order.

And so it is with the Liberal Statists—control is their singular goal and they will seemingly stop at nothing to attain it. Yet the very thing that they grasp for—in the end—becomes, in essence, the very thing that they lose. One cannot exercise control in one's life when such control has been forever ceded to a higher and more dominant power.

"Those whom would sacrifice their Liberties in the interest of security deserve neither and are doomed to lose both."

~Benjamin Franklin

Fractal Insanity: Political Correctness, the Government, and Denial

Week of 11/08/2009

Image 20

We were stunned with the news of an apparent single extremist gunman murdering or wounding in cold blood 42 of our Men and Women in Uniform on the Fort Hood Army Base in Texas. Our thoughts and hearts go out to those members in Fort Hood in particular—but also to our entire Fighting Force in sincere sympathy at both their and our loss during this remembrance period for our Veterans.

We have heard a number of people—both in the Media and otherwise—talk of this loss as being senseless. I, for one, do not view any loss of our soldiers as senseless. These brave men and women gave up their lives in the execution of their duty, whether it be on the battlefield or otherwise. No loss to our military should be counted as senseless, for it demeans the loss of the individual, his or her family and this nation. To a Soldier or Sailor, Airman or Marine, duty is paramount and these men and women made the ultimate sacrifice in their ongoing execution of it.

The killer, we are told, must not be viewed as a terrorist. Nidal Malik Hasan (Foxnews.com, 11/11/2009, "The Complete Notes: Feds Talk About Hasan")? This...man...lies alive and recovering in a soft bed in Texas.

We have read the press releases and heard the Talking Heads indicate to us that this man was a soldier who "snapped" despite having never served in an actual combat environment. We are told that he might have suffered from a new malady, perhaps mutated recently, to give structure to his seemingly inexplicable actions: "Pre-Traumatic Stress Syndrome," which can most likely be likened to "Extreme Cowardice" with regard to how it presents itself in the form of its symptoms.

Political Correctness and Military Duty

Hasan was a Psychiatrist with the rank of Major in the Army. The "Major" was apparently fully trained and educated by the Army during the course of his career. We know that the Major was a Muslim who had ties to

Al-Quaida—those ties apparently having been investigated by our Government and found to be rather harmless and therefore dismissed. In addition, we know that the Major was having a temper tantrum for being required to *actually* serve his country in the Field of Honor for the first time in his long and rather uninspiring career. Nevermind the Major's lack of family or even close friends (beyond certain dancers) that would make going to or near the field of battle difficult. Nevermind the fact that the Major's main job was one of caring for the mental stability of the troops rather than direct or even indirect combat or contact with the enemy.

The Major was apparently a walking, talking diatribe of infantile hypocrisy whom made his extreme Islamic views known to all—even in the process of delivering technical lectures—in the company of his fellows (washingtonpost.com, 11/09/2009, "Fort Hood suspect warned of threats within the ranks"). And when rebutted about his extreme criticisms of our Government with regard to the terrorists which we are fighting against, he became even more distempered and felt hurt and even depressed that his criticism dare be challenged.

The men in his Company, the Army etc., out of extreme and displaced fear of being politically incorrect, apparently did not move to intercept the Major and find out exactly what his major malfunction was.

As a former military man, I still know of and understand the implications that will be brought to bear by overtly and publicly criticizing your country in its endeavors. The old military saying goes: "It's not ours to question why, only ours to do or die." This old adage apparently no longer applies?

I will certainly point up the Men of the Military's view on serving and that is, when one joins up with the military, one temporarily gives up his or her liberties in order that the peoples of the nation might continue with theirs. This is, indeed, the truth—I have been there myself.

Defining the Act and Culpability

I think we all might very much like to know by whose command the investigation into this individual was dismissed. The record is certainly there of who made the determination to dismiss the investigation. Apparently, our Government seems more concerned with who is at political odds with its leadership than with actual threats to its population.

If one looks at the **definition of terrorism** under US Law Code, US Code Title 22,ch.38,paragraph 2656f(d), one will find the following: **"The term terrorism means premeditated, politically motivated violence against noncombatant targets by sub-national groups or clandestine agents"** (history.navy.mil, "Definition of

Terrorism"). The victims, being that they were unarmed, many being medical personnel, would certainly qualify as noncombatant, and the Major, with his disclosed ties to Al Qaeda and an Imam of particular violent notoriety, could easily be determined to be a clandestine agent acting on behalf of our enemies. No one can doubt the political motivation in Hasan's criticism of our actions since 9/11. In addition, the Major purchased two handguns—one in particular of a body armor-piercing configuration—shortly prior to his attack.

Therefore, it would appear that we have suffered our first major Islamic extremist terrorist attack on US Soil since 9/11, and this due primarily to the insanity of political correctness.

Certain folks among and above us will continue in their denial of this truth, but perpetual denial of a particular truth will only make culpability easier to track by history with regard to the action that invokes the denial.

The Poor Marksmen in Our Government

I suppose if this fractally increasing insanity that we are experiencing continues, we will soon, if we have not already, enter the total damnation stage of "what was formerly right is now wrong, and what was formally wrong is now right." We are seeing evidence of this phenomenon already, what with our Government insistently focusing on passage of a Healthcare Act that is certainly not necessary in the face of unemployment numbers that continue their climb. The leadership's preoccupation with this seems to overshadow anything else.

In addition, we have troops in need of help that has yet to come at this writing, not to mention a Stimulus Bill that has proved effective at only stimulating the hyperbole coming out of our Politicans' mouths. This while more and more Americans fall out of work.

Our Mainstream Media seems fixated on telling us only about how right and well things are going—with the exception of our healthcare—which must be far more important to the Media than the economy, despite the fact that it is one of the few sectors within our economy that has seemed to continue its ongoing excellence without fail. In truth, like poor Marksmen, our leadership continually misses the target of the true endeavors for which they have been elected.

We have also seen a Congressional bill voted on in the affirmative that includes language that will require a citizen of this country be jailed in addition to incurring fines if that person fails to purchase healthcare coverage. Now this is an insanity that bars explanation. Illegal aliens within our country, it would appear, are safer from our Government than we ourselves as citizens are—since in being an illegal alien, one will apparently not be required to purchase such coverage since the alien in question is not technically HERE. One then would have to wonder: If a citizen is caught without coverage, can said citizen then renounce his or her citizenship and therefore get around the law were it to pass the Senate?

We might only hope that the geometrically progressing "Insanity of Denial" in political correctness, which seems to infest every nook and cranny in our society and government, is incrementally expunged and that true common sense in our dealings with one another might take hold again. A Genuine Civility in our discourse among differing people is a far more workable solution than the veneer of insincere dismissal of stupendous excess which only encourages a harboring of even more viral and volatile demeanors within a society.

"See What You See"

~Ronald W. Reagan

An Historical Aberration: From Change We Can Believe In To Change We Simply Cannot Believe

Week of 11/15/2009

Image 21

The President recently met with the Japanese Emperor and—yet again—bowed deeply to another Foreign Monarch in greeting.

Now, while the President continues his inane bowing to these Foreign Monarchs (perhaps while mumbling an apology) as if he is the sole star of his own show, no doubt to be called "Bow Watch," we at Conservative Refocus—as well as many of our friends—began to wonder about the exact historical etiquette as it regards US Presidential deference in the form of the custom of

147

bowing to others. We all seem to find it rather odd of our President, and yet we cannot put our finger on the exact reason. This is most likely due to the fact that within our history, no President has typically ever done it (with regard to other Heads of State), and there is a reason for that fact and this reason can be found in the US Constitution.

Why all the hubbub? Well, if one were to look within the American Heritage Dictionary, one would find "bow" as a verb with the following words included within the definition—"to bend downward or to stoop"—along with the meanings which include "greeting, acknowledgment, veneration, submission, to yield in defeat, to yield out of courtesy and to submit." The definition of "bowing" includes seven signs of surrender or servility, and this, I suppose, is our reason for being so negatively picky about the President's obsequiousness in representing our Nation. Not to mention the fact that this, our most traveled President in American history, seems to be flying all over the world in order to strategically practice his Blasted Bow, for goodness sake!

US History of Royal Distaste

In the early days of the Founding, the citizens of the colonies had endured quite enough mistreatment from monarchs who had abused them in myriad ways both in America and, in many cases, in their native countries.

This not to mention the ill treatment and tyrannical practices from religious persecution and otherwise that often drove them to settle in the Americas. As a result, the Founders instituted a government which was intended to defeat deference to any monarchy or religious persuasion. This instinctive dislike of anything that even resembled royalty or forced religious submission is how our forefathers ultimately avoided repeating the mistake of installing a monarchy rather than the rule of law, or Republic, that was finally instated. Yet I should point out that some few among them seemed pensive for royalty despite the problems such an outdated system offered. This mindset can, even now, be seen among many of the Liberals and personally challenged "innocents" that we find in office, if not in the populace, in the form of "figuratively" crowning our President "the Messiah" in his treatment, if not in their blindingly ideological universal acceptance of him and his "ideas." I can even recall one mentally challenged Liberal pundit referring to the Prez as "Godlike" in his dispassionate manner, for Heaven's sake, and let's not forget the "thrill up Chris Matthew's leg"—Egad!

In Article 1 Section 9 of the US Constitution, one will find the following: *No Title of Nobility shall be granted by the United States: And no Person holding any Office of Profit or Trust under them, shall, without the Consent of the Congress, accept of any present, Emolument.*

Office, or Title, of any kind whatever, from any King, Prince or foreign State.

Now some might argue that this would apply only to our government; however, the reasoning seems very clear within the Freedom Charters that the US had the intent of universally rendering invalid any title of nobility as we believe that "all men are created equal." This does not mean that American Government did not recognize the authority of other monarchs to govern their own people—just that our Forefathers did not recognize any sort of silly individual supremacy over others which might be claimed by Royalty.

In addition, as soon as the Founders wrote those powerful words concerning the "equality of all men," then slavery had to, imperatively, be on the way out as it flew in the face of our stated principles as so set forth by the Founder's own words. And so it was that slavery was eventually abolished, although it took 90 more years and a horrendous war (with regard to State's rights in conjunction with slavery) to finally and thankfully eradicate it from the land.

Well-Educated, Clueless and Sneaky

Now, as our "learned and well-educated" leaders might obviously know of all this history, one might think that the White House had learned its lesson when only back in April 2009 the Prez initiated a bow to the Saudi King that caused quite a bit of an uproar. The White House, in usual form, desperately—if not defensively—argued that "it was not a bow" despite video clearly showing that **it was a bow** or perhaps an extreme bout of "stomach cramps" that had obviously doubled the President over at the worst of all possible times (come on guys—at least try to be creative!). The Brits were probably in a snit that the President failed to bow to their Queen on his UK visit and yet would generously bow to "male" Saudi dictators. In addition, the Saudis, according to Saudi newspaper accounts, were also "pleasantly pleased" that the Prez proffered a zesty bow to their Glorious King, which had been overdue for some time...apparently.

We have also seen, in our research, several rather hysterical arguments that President Bush had also bowed to the Saudi King in the recent past—which we would have dutifully reported in this article if he actually had. However, in a CNN video we find that Bush had bowed his head to the rather short in stature Saudi King so that the King could place a "really cool medallion" around Bush's neck.

Those Liberals! While not very bright, they are cunning and sneaky and bear considerable watching, one must declare.

The Internet result of every bit of research that we have done concludes that NO US President has ever bowed to any foreign leadership on this earth for over 230 years (which is as it should be)—until now.

Entertaining the World and a New Hope for Aluminum Chlorohydrate

In our history, George Washington did initially hold Levees with US Men of Prominence (a holdover from the old English Court System) in which they initially bowed to the President while standing in a semi-circle (thus the Oval Office), and then the President would address each individual in person and bow in return to each (see the White House Historical Association website). Thomas Jefferson, my personal favorite, ended the etiquette of bowing by judiciously shaking hands with all, and thus the bow had forever been broken. Well, at least—once again—until now.

With the gravity that the H1N1 has brought to the fore of Presidential politics, perhaps Obama should now blaze a new trail and start coughing beneath his armpit in greeting foreign dignitaries. He can then slow the tide of the terrible virulent onslaught while changing the Jeffersonian practice of handshaking to the "avant-garde armpit coughing" that his administration finds so endearing.

Presidential greeting by way of armpit coughing. Now that's change we can actually believe in—in that is not harmful to the country beyond the goodwill engendering peals of laughter that we would most definitely receive from other nations.

But at least it beats bowing...

"I cannot teach you violence as I do not myself believe in it. I can only teach you not to bow your heads before anyone even at the cost of your life."

~Mahatma Gandhi

The Political Richter Scale: Measuring The Continental Shift in Ideologies

Week of 11/22/2009

Image 22

This week we begin our national period of Thanksgiving, which seems ironic when looking back on the events of this past week. We have had so many depressingly newsworthy issues going on across so many fronts it would seem that one could throw a stick in any direction and hit an important if not fascinating development that had just occurred. The unemployment rate has twittered upward yet again along with mortgage foreclosures and delinquencies (great job so far President Obama!).

At Conservative Refocus, we cannot help but revisit a much earlier article ("The Case for Capitalism: The

Statist Menace") that was written with regard to our economic positioning during this period of great financial unrest, if not distress. In retrospect, my initial concern of some time ago with regard to writing this column and finding a sufficiency of things of both importance and singular interest to warrant the time-involved writing effort (it would seem) were both grossly and rather amusingly overstated.

To wit—I should point out that when we at Conservative Refocus, just a scant three months ago, began writing about issues that we thought were of great import (but were not receiving adequate and objective media attention), we had no idea that we would reach nearly one million readers in such a short time frame—ranking us within the top 5% of all of the websites on the planet—and we have you to thank for this, and we appreciate your time and effort in reading our soft-rants.

Out of the Mouths of Babes (No...Not You Norah)

Regardless—the most important issue that has percolated up this past week (much like raw sewage from a malfunctioning septic system) has been the Senate's acceptance vote to begin deliberations on the "pungent" Senate Healthscare Bill. In addition to that, we have MSNBC reporter Norah O'Donnell intrepidly attempting to engage in debate on national TV a young 17 year old girl standing in line at a Sarah Palin book signing event.

Little did Norah know that she was engaging a young Constitutional Expert–"bless Norah's heart."

One half expected the young Conservative lady in completion of her quick dissertation, which filled me with great pride, to end the mini-debate with a triple-twisting back flip and perfect landing. For me personally, Norah, all things being equal—I would never engage a youngling "Socialist" in "debate ambush format" on national television simply to debase and embarrass them, but it would seem your personal comeuppance was delivered threefold—we noted also that the MSNBC clip has now been "really clipped" removing the young lady's thorough rebuttal to Norah—forcing us to search for and find a new clip (nah-na-nah-nah na). *See YouTube.com, 11/18/2009, "Norah O'Donnell Grills a Young Girl for Her Support of Sarah Palin."

We have also seen the anniversary of the tearing down of the Berlin Wall, which was, ironically, covered by every major Mainstream Media network. The networks in their covering of these events—and in a misleading spate of revisionism—made little if any mention of President Reagan's admonition at the exact Berlin location to Soviet President Gorbachev to "tear down that wall."

Ladies and Gentlemen, it was Reagan's words and actions that culminated the event.

I find it rather galling that the networks were celebrating Germany's freedom and reunification while, at the same time, in essence, "being Culpables-in-Chief" over the Government's attempts at the demise of our own freedom in their slanted if not nonexistent critical efforts. Now, what was that about the *myth* of the Liberal Media?

With regard to the Healthcare Bill—I have been reminding everyone possible—who seemed in a near-panic afterward—that the vote which has been passed was simply a figurative "go-ahead" for the deliberations to begin—meaning we need not panic and essentially run for the bomb-shelters just yet. But it does bear considerable alarm as we watch Harry "the Lumberjack" Reid's continuing impressive efforts to pulp every tree in America by Congressional publication fiat.

The thing to remember is that one complete bill has to be passed by both the Senate and the House before the cursed thing becomes law, and there is much that must be done in order to squeeze the two current, separate bills of deformed legislation together into the one bill and then get it passed. By the way, and with regard to Harry Reid, if you would like to see and hear our true opinion of both he and his ongoing Senatorial efforts, you need only see Dennis Miller's hilarious rant that pretty much covers our complete sentiments in this regard (youtube.com, 06/11/2009, "Dennis Miller Rips Harry Reid a New One").

So How Many Democrats Does It Take to Screw in a Lightbulb?

While watching the Senate debate on 11/21, our Conservative Refocus Researcher/Producer, Kim Stallings, brought up several excellent observations concerning the proceedings. Kim's first impression was that the Senate Democrats—in their stream of incessant speeches extolling the virtues of their warped and stunted legislation—did so with a constant smirk on their respective faces as if it were all great fun and mischief, "building their case based upon emotional manipulation and pathos" while dragging out singular instances of arguable individual cases that appealed to the heart. Such emotional appeals are often deceitful and divert an audience from the actual logic of the debate. In addition, she indicated that their prose was actually quite clumsy and rather disingenuous as if they were "gleefully oblivious" to be cramming the bill down the throats of the Republicans, the few Democratic Statesmen, and, in reality, the American People.

Kim further pointed out that the Republicans, "standing strong in great contrast to the Democrats, were speaking forcefully and addressing each and every point with clear logic in eloquent and powerful opposition to the bill," while supporting their arguments with sound evidence. Meanwhile the American People during this time are trying to recover from the figurative "Waterboarding

Act" that the Liberal Statist members of the government have performed on them by way of all of this legislative nonsense that seems to have become Gospel to the "Government Leaders" but anathema to our respective Liberties.

While I simply could not bear to watch our hard fought for liberties being mangled by the leering Democratic Court Jesters within our government, I would be remiss if I did not point out to you my empathic sense of this entire process. While all of this is going on, we cannot help but in sensitivity feel and see the panicked yet silent sweat oozing off the brows of the Democrats and the wide-eyed hysteria they emote like a cornered and imperiled creature who knows his end is at hand.

The Seismic Shift

The Washington Democrats, in playing out their macabre act upon the stage, have telegraphed to a great many of the American People one simple and true fact and that is the conviction that many within the populace who thought themselves moderate Democrats actually find themselves to be Independents and many who thought themselves Lite Democrats find themselves to be Liberal Republicans. Further, many who thought of themselves as Liberal Republicans now might think of themselves as moderate Republicans and so on and so forth. In other words the Democrats, by way of their own radical actions, have elicited a seismic shift within the entire political ideological spectrum of the United States and the bellwether of this result will be seen in the next 12 months by way of the elections. Most people simply do not wish to be associated with—dare I say it?—Hell's Bells why not!—"The Party of the Insane" and their total debasement of Constitutional principles as if the Bill of Rights were nothing more than a worthless advertising flyer that found its way into their line of sight and then promptly into the nearest waste can.

While none should ever take any of these proceedings lightly, there are a multitude of silver linings associated with all of these dark and ominous storm clouds that are seemingly menacing us from every direction, and I will joyfully entertain you as to my reasoning if you will but hear me out.

The populace in their past and pacifistic somber of disdain with regard to "all things politic" can finally see what happens when one removes and disengages his hand from the brake of the "massive locomotive" that is our country, as the true and great Ronald Reagan once put it. We can all see that a Republic, no matter how economically strong and viable, no matter how rigid its seeming-democratic controls, no matter how responsible and good natured, its constituents can easily if not unwittingly become victim to ideological sophistry and find itself terribly weakened and vulnerable to the point of folding in on itself, on and by way of, its own strengths.

That we have seen and now learned of this weakness by way of a Tri-convergent Liberal Storm—Legislative, Executive and Media—will most likely and in many ways inoculate us to any "near" future permutations (assuming our prediction holds true). In addition, the Media, in its own brand of sophistry, has found itself weakened by its disregard of/love of radical left-wingism that the people, its readers and buyers, do not accept and therefore look increasingly to other sources for social and political information.

Fun with Bill, Hillary and John

We are also seeing "A Continental Shift" back towards the Constitution and its champions of the past—the Conservative Republicans. The next election cycle will most likely bring about a large shift, and then another major shift in the next election after that, which will make repeal of any current Liberty incursions that may be passed a very strong if not inexorable conclusion to all of these unholy legislative acts. In fact, we should, even now, be repealing the Stimulus due to its impotence that has stimulated nothing but our future deficits.

The old saying that we have all heard, "There's not a dime's worth of difference between a Republican and a Democrat" can now easily be found to be totally worthless and laughable as the most inane quote of the century. This despite the fact that some few Democrats, Joseph Lieberman comes to mind, whom still hold out their Democratic versus Republican principles while heroically trying to slam the brakes on the idiocy that the Senator finds within his own party, still speak well for the Democratic signets that have in the past marked a healthy contrast of diversity within our body politic. But when a party's slight breeze becomes a gale (if not a hurricane) of extremism, we can then all see the stark differences between the two.

You know things are bad when, as a Conservative, you find yourself wistfully wishing—if we **must** have a Democrat—for Bill or Hillary or even John Edwards, for Heaven's sake—someone that holds the history of this country's principles in at least a semblance of high regard.

Image 23

You have no idea, Mr. President....

Refutation to the Editorial "The Phantom Menace" by Paul Krugman

Week of 11/22/2009

Image 24

No, Mr. Krugman, it's "The **Statist** Menace," and yes, I would agree with at least one thing within your article and that is we are, indeed, on our way to the "new" New Deal, and it is one that essentially taxes the bejesus out of us all in order to set into "clunky" motion economic principles which belong in the garbage heap of history rather than the much ballyhooed "Change We Can Believe In" mantra that seems to be bankrupting our country.

I am still trying to figure out how the "Statesmen" that are referred to in this article as the "Centrists" in the

Senate are hobbling efforts to rescue the economy? The only thing we have seen that has hit a possible passage roadblock is the Senate Healthcare Bill. I fail to see how a budget-busting piece of legislation is going to help the economy. By that reasoning—perhaps we should all turn our ceiling fans on so that we can lower the global temperatures even further than they have already declined in the midst of this "phantom global warming" that the Liberals love to proudly parade around like a mannequin with lipstick on—that we are then supposed to take seriously....Oh, yes! Quite a lovely lady she is, Sir...(for Heaven's sake).

Paul then drags out "leading Economist" Lawrence Summers who had called for decisive action towards the economy in December of 2008 stating "doing too little poses a greater threat than doing too much," which is now a moot point because nothing has really been done for the better part of this year beyond a great deal of talking.

Paul goes on to point out that most Economists he talks to believe that "the big risk to recovery comes from the inadequacy of government efforts." Paul states that "the stimulus was too small and it will fade out next year while higher unemployment is undermining consumer and business confidence."

Excuse me Paul, but please allow me to point out the following: **The reason the Stimulus is not working so far is because only 28% of the funds have been allocated and have only just now kicked in.**

That's right, Ladies and Gentlemen. The total amount that has been paid out at the time of this writing is only $220 Billion. We have a $14 Trillion dollar economy and $220 Billion amounts to less than a pinprick to a $14 Trillion dollar economy—even if it were to work, it has not yet had a chance to. If we do a considerable amount of rounding we could say that the Stimulus equals almost $1 Trillion for comparison purposes. This means that the Stimulus represents without the rounding less than 6% of our total economy even after the entire Stimulus has been paid out.

Now, let's look at this problem by comparing these values in the terms of a household in the US that makes $50,000 per year—let's multiply $50,000 times that same 6% and see what we get. The answer is $3,000. Granted that's nice and it works out to about double what President Bush gave to most tax-paying families in 2007. But the problem is the following: If we compare our family values to the US economy—this would mean that these same tax-paying families have so far only received 28% or $840. Now remember this is just for comparison since families are not actually getting this— the entities actually receiving these funds were essentially hand-picked by the fine folks in our Government.

At any rate, if you are trying to clothe your family, make house payments, eat, etc., that same $840 over a year's time would amount to about $70.00 per month, **which might pay a freaking cable bill!** That's right. So the answer to this, according to Paul, is to throw more money at the problem despite the fact that very little has actually been thrown at the problem so far. (The Liberal brain is, apparently, a mystery that defies explanation.)

Further, the true aim of a Stimulus is to actually "stimulate" –this has actually been more of a tease than a stimulation. If this measure were actually going to work, would not a better solution be to give that money directly to the families so that the stimulation can felt by everyone and everything within the economy rather than those whom have pleased the Democrats so that they will direct funds their way?

Paul continues on, bemoaning the fact that Obama is (finally and correctly) worrying about deficits rather than stimulating growth, but both I and Professor Walter Williams would submit that the money that the Government is spending is actually sucking private capital out of the market, which is actually exacerbating the problem rather than fixing it.

Paul goes on to explain a few other things that make groundless points at best, but then finishes with the following, which invokes a certain deja' vu: "it's much riskier to do too little that too do too much" and "it's sad and unfortunate that the administration appears to have lost sight of that truth."

My question to that would be, *which* truth are you speaking of that the Administration has lost sight of?

I can only point out that I have yet to see *any* meaningful truth come out of this administration so far, Paul.

Global Warming Meltdown: An Academian Army of Avaricious Chicken Littles throughout History

Week of 11/29/2009

Image 25

Last week may have seen an amusing and yet important turning point in the global warming debate that many Conservatives, including this one, have constantly questioned over many, many years—after a computer hacker barged his or her way into the Hadley Research Center which is located in Great Britain (see climate-gate.com). The Center is considered one of the linchpins of the International Community's IPCC research on global warming along with East Anglia.

The industrious hacker downloaded a prodigious amount of emails from both researchers and directors that plainly revealed that the (no doubt now) really "Mad Scientists" were intentionally hiding data that would have proved damning to their entire reason for a rather expensive existence on the world's dole. President Obama, whose energy policy along with Cap and Trade legislation hinges on the dire urgency of global warming, upon hearing of this news promptly decided that an earlier decision to forego his climate meeting in Copenhagen be "rethought." Now Obama will apparently be rushing to the "important" climate meeting in order to perform "Global Damage Control," and perhaps in true Messiah fashion, "resurrect" the recently deceased issue of global warming as far as these illuminating emails are concerned.

The Conservative Mindset on Most Things Global

By way of explanation as to "thinking" Conservatives, and the reason that so many of us have questioned the veracity of the "pop science" that is manmade global warming—seems more grounded in our critical observation of history along with the constant deluge of the multi-generational Liberal hobby of trying to "scare the spoor" out of the population into conforming (those around them) to their mind-numbed, lock step, Utopian approach to life in general. One must remember that some of the greedy Chicken Littles in Academia often need more than just the teaching of our young in order to be fulfilled within their already rather important profession of its own accord. All too often, Liberal Academians seem to think of themselves also as "Human Pavlovian Programmers" in downloading, not just critical thinking and problem solving skills, but also "near computer virus-like" brain trojans which seem to automatically jolt the trained students back into Academia's puppet-master fold when the youngsters try to wander off into "Logical Land"—which must be no more than Bizzaro World to these Liberal Academian Maestros.

Here at Conservative Refocus, as always, rather than attempting to talk one into our reasoning—as do the constantly jabbering Statists—we prefer to show and prove why we see these things as we do—so why not take a look at some of the media-driven, manmade, and natural disaster specters that have buggered us over the years, ultimately proving to be nothing more than an often audaciously expensive flight of fancy before we dive into our perspective on the "researchers'" data.

The Global Cooling Scare of the Early to Mid 70s

In the early 1970s, the Media became incensed at the possibility of global cooling and that we might indeed be entering into a climate cyclical ice age. An actual newspaper article dated 5/21/75 from (ahem) The New

York Times, "Scientists Ask Why World Climate Is Changing; Major Cooling May Be Ahead," put forth the dire possibility of all of us needing to grow a plush layer of fur as a result of either manmade pollution—yet again—or solar energy variations (gets my vote) or theoretical orbital oscillations (perhaps) or even volcanic eruptions which have actually now been proven to reduce prolonged global temperatures by nearly a degree in some instances.

Image 26

The interesting thing about this particular article is that many of the facts within it seem to have been recycled into the current "hypothesis" regarding global warming. In essence, the same instances that are blamed for causing global warming were also attributed, in this 1975 article, to the postulated global cooling. Many have surmised, even now, that our main and true concern might be towards global cooling and how it might affect world food stores as a result of vastly shortened growing seasons. Amusingly, this 1975 article indicates that our artificial production of greenhouse gasses may actually be keeping the global cooling at bay. So can we now purchase a Humvee without all of the combat environmentalists flipping the bird at us (at best) since we may actually be saving the planet?

The Forever but Never Oil Shortage of the Late 70s

As early as 1874, some began fretting that oil would soon run out. In 1914, the "experts" within our government indicated that we had only a 10 year supply remaining. In 1940, once again, the government indicated that we then had only a 15 year supply remaining. In 1977, the ostensibly rather unbrilliant Jimmy Carter indicated that foreign oil, in 15 years, would be too pricey for our country to afford. Even then Carter saw the need to develop our own resources and that the situation, at that time, seemed dire. Yet today we refuse to drill in diverse and even barren environs due chiefly to the impact of the ardent environmentalists who seem to wish us to live in profligate misery—if we were to adopt every one of their uber-primitive Marxist-inspired issues and live by them.

The simple fact is that oil can be found in so many places via so many means of expertise that no one can actually say if we might ever run out of the stuff. It was recently determined that oil shale, which was found in huge deposits in Wyoming, Utah and Colorado, but also in other areas of the world, contains enough oil to power the United States for generations to come to the tune of at least 2.7 trillion barrels. The vagaries and extremes that have harmed our economy in the pricing of oil and its byproducts have more to do with self-imposed boundaries on refining and drilling limitations than anything else. Many scientists agree that oil actually comes from single-celled microscopic creatures called *diatoms* which live by converting solar energy into their own nourishment—that being oil—naturally produced by their bodies.

Image 27

These tiny creatures have been around for millions if not billions of years and—even now---float around in virtually every aquatic environment known to man. The oil that we retrieve from their past existence is what fuels our engines of society. From death comes life, it would seem even here.

The Ozone Hole Scare of the 1980s

In the mid-80s, our now proliferate satellite technology allowed us to be able to view our atmosphere and earth on a scale, of course, never before seen by Man. The result of this, rather than the "radiant enlightenment" one might expect from scientific advances, was an apocalyptic scare of mammoth proportions in the form of a polar ozone hole that scientists were able to alarmingly observe on a newly continual basis.

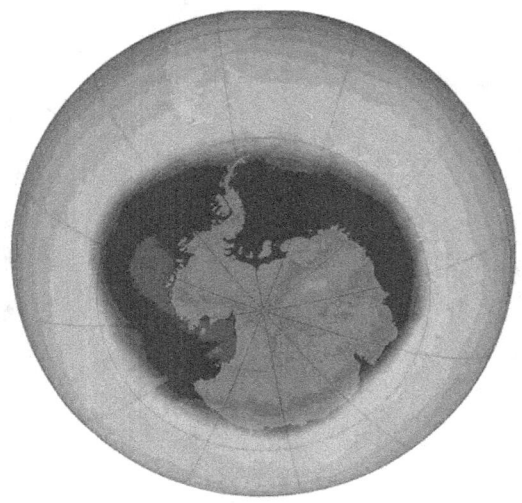

Image 28

Rather than levelheadedly acknowledging that—having been unable to view this phenomenon before—perhaps we should simply observe and study in a scientific manner—the Liberal Media, predictably, reacted with hysterics.

Ozone is a gaseous particle that, in this case, aids in blocking harmful ultraviolet radiation from the earth's surface. The Media was relentless in its typical kneejerk reaction, and before long virtually every government in the world was passing laws and new regulations designed to combat the sinister advances of a newly found Gaseous Criminal identified as the chlorofluorocarbon found in Freon—which has a delimiting effect on ozone. The CFC gases which are used en mass by every nation in the world—most commonly as an air conditioning refrigerant—were denigrated even to the point of efforts to eliminate the life saving asthma inhibiting inhalers used by asthmatics in order to clear their airways when an asthma attack sets in (Associated Press, 2006, "FDA Panel Called for Ban on Some OTC Inhalers"). The staggering monetary figure which the world spent in order to reduce and eventually eliminate this type of Freon, as it turns out, was a total waste in resources—nevermind the volume of CFC's that volcanoes routinely spew out.

In modern days we now find that the hole in the ozone layer is, indeed, cyclical in its nature, and that ozone is constantly created and destroyed by the interaction between sunlight and oxygen. The final result of all of this was better than a decade of a total waste of money, intellect and abject fear. Does this, perhaps, remind you of anything going on currently?

The AIDS Pandemic that Wasn't

Also in the 80s was the scourge of AIDS or Acquired Immune Deficiency Syndrome. This virus, which begins as HIV—and which has also been accused as being manmade by many conspiracy theorists—attacks the immune system in such a way as to render it nearly powerless to combat other maladies after a time of lying dormant.

Once news of this pandemic reached Mainstream Media, we were all appropriately ashen at the fact that the primary means of transference of this virus was by sexual contact and that there was no known cure. Suddenly, instead of being rendered uncomfortable for a time as a result of one's sexual proclivities, a person could die from his or her erotic excesses, for Heaven's sake! The Media was once again profligate in its reaction, detailing a Black-Death-type of mortality rate that might eventually wipe out entire populations.

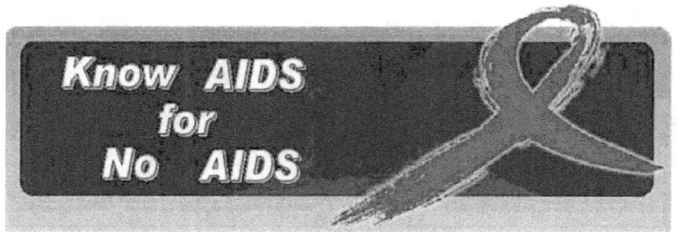

Image 29

The fact that the virus was most commonly associated with homosexuals and intravenous drug users only excited the Media and Liberals even more.

It should be pointed out that the disease was, indeed, a terrible scourge to the aforementioned populations and many of us knew or still know some whom have fallen ill and/or expired from this terrible infection; however, the transference to general populations as a whole was never actually realized (policynetwork.net, 01/2008, "The Myth of a General AIDS Pandemic: How billions are wasted on unnecessary AIDS prevention programmes"). Even the disease's world predominance in sub-Saharan populations has been overstated by as much as 50%, some studies cite, in addition to the countless articles and books that have been written dealing with the same grossly overstated instances of world hysteria as associated with the other apocalypses already noted within this article.

The Myth of Deforestation and Manmade Species Extinction

In addition to the already debunked items that would have seen the human race eventually expunged, we also have the myths of deforestation and the property rights eviscerating "Endangered Species Act" that has become nothing more than a political tool designed to extract property from individuals when no other way appears to exist by the members of both local and Statist Government. With regard to the touted deforestation problems, in actuality, the US has reduced its forest only from 45% to 33% since the Pilgrims first set foot on the

North American continent, and much of this is used to grow crops.

In addition, since 1920, according to the US Department of Agriculture, forested land has actually remained about equal.

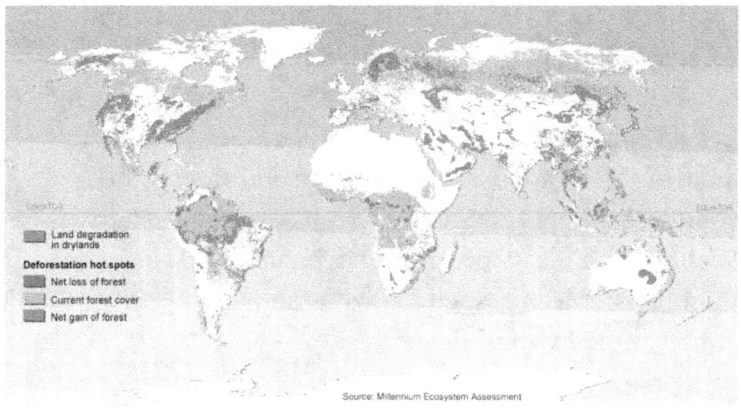

Image 30

Species, on the other hand, have come and gone over millions of years and our efforts to control and increase a particular species seems all too often to come at the expense of unsuspecting property owners—in many cases doing more harm than good.

There are indeed instances of species being nearly hunted to extinction, but in these cases, no one can actually know for sure how many members of a particular species exist in the oceans or the environment.

We had one particular article earlier this year (SFGate.com, 03/03/2009, "Overfishing imperils ocean life, study says")"which indicated that the oceans were being decimated of fish by fishermen. This article was later recanted (msnbc.com, 07/31/2009, "Sustainable seas? Overfishing easing in places") but without nearly the sensational forthrightness of the earlier article (of course). In fact, the US can't even keep track of illegals within its borders—so then how can it, in truth, keep track of the various species that occupy the largely unexplored watery depths of 90% of the earth's total area?

The Damning Details in the Global Warming Researchers' Emails

In our perusing through the emails available (Wall Street Journal, 11/25/2009, "Climate Science and Candor"), the one singular fact that keeps surfacing is the consternation the researchers seem to show with regard to how to parse the data between what appeared to be global cooling or neutrality at best and their aim to substantiate Global Warming. The emails discuss blips and, long what we have always suspected, their ability to skew the data with fractional adjustments (by inserting false but difficult to catch numbers into their research equations) working to their favor in efforts to prove warming.

The researchers also seemed baffled in the oscillations between the NH (Northern Hemisphere) and the SH (Southern Hemisphere) or blips (blips in this inference can be attributed to data that does not fit in with their agenda). In addition to that, we also frequently see the researchers refer to "problems" within the data set. Once again—problems in this venue can be attributable to evidence which simply does not fit in with the researchers' aim to prove global warming.

The nail in the coffin would have to be, in this case, the researchers' email which essentially bemoans the new UK Freedom of Information Act, and also purports to hide behind a Data Protection Act, despite the fact that the data was apparently government/publicly funded. Additionally, the final email instructs the receiver to delete all emails—this blatantly points to a fear of the details behind the research data being known. Also of great concern is the fact that the global data as being researched was withheld from Peer Review, despite the fact that in bringing to fruition the hypothesis of manmade carbon proliferations as being culpable to global warming, one must have a general acceptance among one's scientific peers in order that the subject be brought from the standard transition of hypothesis to theory to accepted scientific fact. No such progression has yet been made. And yet here we have the—in large part—quasi-Socialist governments of the world insisting on bringing the US in as a leader in "Global Warming Correction" in the form of "payola" to other third world nations for "participation" (in addition to the rampant energy taxes that will be brought into existence domestically through Cap and Trade legislation once these damnable items have been made into law—were that to tragically occur).

Is this Just the Tip of the "Single Remaining" Iceberg?

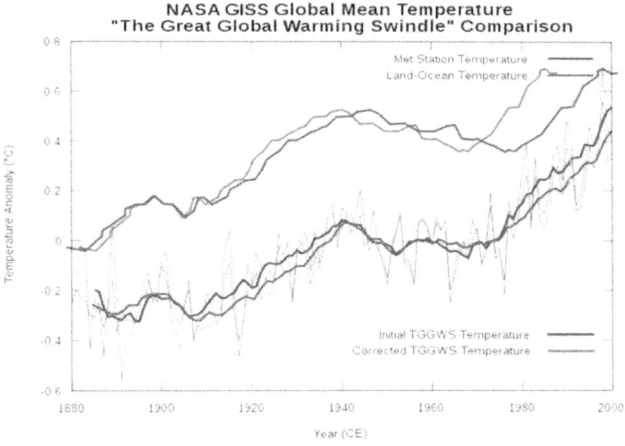

Image 31

In addition—as this article is being written—more information seems to be continually spilling out that convicts certain members of the Media of withholding information that is beyond damning to their cause in support of global warming. In fact, the latest news states that when these emails were initially hacked from Hadley—apparently one month ago—they were then promptly sent to several major Media outlets within the UK. These outlets, rather than being outraged at the research facility for the obviously manufactured numbers being used to perpetuate the global warming myth, chose to sit on the data and keep quiet—no doubt hoping blithely that the entire issue would pass.

We can expect this may have also occurred in Mainstream Media outlets within the US. The irony, however, continues as many of you may have noticed— as the truth about global warming continually leaches out—you most likely have also seen your daily newspaper "dry heave" up various articles in connection with the Hadley email leakage stories that point, for instance, to the skiing industry being hurt by unseasonably warm temperatures in various areas (implying that global warming is happening and hurting us)—as is always the case each year within regions, for Heaven's sake. We have also seen research presented at the "4 Degrees and Beyond, International Climate Science Conference" at the University of Oxford which indicates that only 10% of the entire population will survive if temperatures increase by 4 degrees Celsius, telling us that "the results will be terrifying," which should make most environmentalists ecstatic from what we have seen (commondreams.org, 10/09/2009, "Four Degrees of Devastation").

The question that we as Americans should be asking of our Senators and State Representatives and any other politician—whether they wish to listen or not—is simply this: Apparently, as of this writing, **if there is, indeed, to be a *serious* Congressional investigation into all of this false and misleading data with regard to global warming and the pending Cap and Trade legislation, should not all current legislation be suspended indefinitely?** It now seems obvious that the costly changes and taxes, which are most definitely forthcoming, are based on an illusion that is designed to chain us, as well as citizens of other countries, to a set of regulations and laws that further degrade and imperil the economies and remaining liberties of the developed world.

Is pursuit of the simple truth in all things now so damaging to the contrived constructs of our respective governments that we must now live in a false matrix of perception? The question then becomes "Why do governments consistently buy into these phenomena when they are more often than not proven to be false?"

No doubt we have only just scratched the surface with this writing, but we expect to pay a number of visits to this subject in the near and foreseeable future.

Rebuttal to Thomas Friedman's Article "Some Are Confused, or Just in Denial"

Week of 11/29/2009

Image 32

While I have sometimes enjoyed reading Thomas Friedman, I could not help but take issue with his editorial piece concerning global warming and his opposition to the drill-baby-drill proponents who simply wish to see a secure America, which may face an uncertain economic future if world energy instability were to rear its often-seen and grotesque head.

Of Doves and Energy

History has taught us that extreme energy dependence on other countries is a practice which is fraught with ill consequences, and, like it or not, the technology that is required to power our various engines of society sans oil is simply unavailable on a practical basis as of yet. One

189

need only take a strong and hard look at the origins of World War II to see that energy availability was one of the cornerstones of our poor relations with Japan, not to mention Japan's rampant Imperialism at the time. One has to wonder if Friedman actually thinks that we have progressed so far since those dim days of the early 40's that we have now surpassed ourselves and are above waging war over energy? I wouldn't bet on that, Mr. Friedman.

In addition, perhaps Friedman sees himself as leaning towards Conservatism, but after reading this particular article I am not quite sure what type of Conservatism that might be. The New York Times brand maybe? Trotting out and being in favor of the tyrannical measures and economic bruising that is the Cap and Trade tax is not exactly what we would consider to be a Conservative value. As a matter of fact, those values belong more on the Liberal side of the aisle than anywhere else.

With regard to the contention that Conservatives believe in a black-plague-type malady by 2050...um...now which Conservatives would those be, Sir? That sort of natural disaster mindset is typified by the Liberals in our midst rather than Conservatives—you know, the ones who have been raising everyone's hackles over the dreaded global warming that is coming (only to a movie house near you, perhaps, as it would now seem).

Facts versus Beliefs

Or maybe the now "Messiah-influenced inner beltway" environs, in addition to the Northeast, have been altered to the point of rebranding the entire spectrum of the Left into factions where a new middle point has now been fashioned! The extreme Marxist Left is now simply Moderate and the Center Left would then be Conservative, I suppose. Further, now anything that is actually to right of the "old-fashioned" center is considered Radical Right-Wing and bears no serious consideration. (I am certain that a host of both Republican Senators and Congressman would agree in part with this hypothesis).

Friedman goes on to point out that "many of us believe that it is much better for America that the world be dependent on oil for energy?" Um...it is certainly not a question of what we do or do not believe but rather a statement of mere fact, Sir, that the world is dependent upon oil for energy, and I do not see that as being good for America (unless we really start drilling).

I would have to point out that unless we can create a harness which will convert all of the hot air and misinformation pouring out of the Liberals in our government into a usable fuel source then, at least for the moment, oil is the still the cheapest and most plentiful fuel source available.

Get over it. Drill for it. Own it.

The natural marketplace forces that exist will respond appropriately as better technology and cleaner and cheaper fuels come into play. We understand that pollution is an issue—this is why we have continually more efficient cars and trucks that pollute far less. However, **forcing the market to do things that go against sound business practice produces unsound business results.** It's simply that simple. The financial meltdown that we are still suffering is a direct result of what happens when government meddles too deeply within a given market.

Running Water and Bean Sprouts

Friedman then points out that there are certain of those who believe that "folks in the developing world are very happy being poor—just give them a little running water and electricity and they'll be fine—they'll never want to live like us." Now what in the Sam Hill do people in other countries have to do with our energy policy, for Heaven's sake? OK, I feel bad—very bad, now. Isn't that how I am supposed to feel? How dare we strive to make ourselves better when there are people suffering in other countries! (I will, now for certain, eat all of my bean sprouts for supper.) Good Grief! We, Sir, are having enough trouble, it would seem, taking care of ourselves at this point. Are we now to be responsible for the entire undeveloped world as well?

Friedman then points out, among other things, that the world population is increasing to the point where the existing foodstuffs and energy supplies will be inadequate (to paraphrase); therefore, Mr. Friedman, I suppose we will apparently soon start tumbling off of the planet as if it were a huge and crowded subway platform. This mindset is typical for people who spend "way" too much time in large metropolises, I suppose. The real other-world in the Red States, Mr. Friedman, has plenty of room to spare. Perhaps China is growing unhealthily along with some of the other larger populations, but of late we seem to have been reading of European populations becoming stagnant to the point of regression. I suppose the world governments should all now produce legislation requiring briefs rather than boxers?

Worrying over various populations growing too large is, kind of like worrying about whether that hangnail you have is going to become infected *and if so* may cause gangrene *and if so* may cause blood poisoning *and if so* may need to be amputated *and if then* the blood poisoning gets into your heart you could die. (This guy ain't the life of the party, it would seem).

The Green Hawk Meets E.T.

Finally, Friedman moves into "the world is getting flatter" stage. From depression to geographical regression, it would seem. Flatter in this usage actually means people are seeing how other people (i.e. Americans) are living and wish to live that way as well. The world has always been getting flatter, to use your terminology, Mr. Friedman. This is also referred to as progress by many and is actually to be sought after rather than bemoaned.

Mr. Friedman actually then states "I am a **Green Hawk**!" with regard to cleaner burning fuels and alternate energies. Ok....more power to you, Sir. Do you, like, get up and war-paint your face in those Green Hawk colors and strip down to your waist before going to work each day? (I saw a Seinfeld episode about your type once.)

Mr. Friedman continues sowing his wild Cap and Trade seeds in conjunction with Energy Technology—or E.T. as he terms it. Well, I can only point out that E.T. needs to phone home because these workable technology solutions aren't quite here yet, and no amount of ranting is going to bring them here until we have progressed far enough to make it all workable...shouldn't be long but can you exercise a little patience and show a little common sense until then please?

Friedman then actually finishes up with the following quote: "So, as I said, you don't believe in Global Warming? You're wrong!" Very well, Mr. Friedman, I often get tired also at the end of writing a column—they can be exhausting no doubt—so I will end mine with a bit of (surprise!) recycling.

My response to your ending remarks is very simple.

No, Mr. Friedman, according to a bunch of hoaxers that are working in the UK and elsewhere and hiding information that speaks of a decline in global temperatures—You, Sir, are proven wrong!

(Some are confused, or just in denial...)

A New World Religious Order: The Faithful Anthropomorphic Global Warming Sect

Week of 12/06/2009

Image 33

This past week the President finally made a decision that was both highly anticipated and thoroughly dreaded, based on the President's "exemplary" procrastination skills, with regard to Troop deployment in Afghanistan. That the Prez elected to make his speech regarding his decision in front of the West Point Cadets was a wily masterstroke by the President's handlers since the President is so completely adored by our military.

The Event Horizon of this speech was the fact that the President made a valiant if not vain effort to serve two counterpoints, that being those hawks who say that the

President should deliver all the troops that the Generals requested, and the other group—or pacifists—who say that the President needs to pull out all forces or keep them minimal. Both groups, it would seem, got their wish in one hand and their fecal matter in the other. The President correctly granted 30,000 of the 40,000 requested troops to begin deploying nearly immediately.

Song of Solomon

On the other hand, the President, in an attempt at partially appeasing his Liberal supporters, indicated that the troops' deadline to get the job done was 18 months and then they were to be pulled out. Just think of this as the military deployment version of the game show "Jeopardy," one should suppose (no pun intended). Thus, in one fell swoop, the President, in true Solomon-like fashion, "split the baby in half."

The result of all of this was a cacophony of derangement from the Administration which ultimately resulted in a really weird game of Good Cop/Bad Cop. The Administration's apparatchiks (thanks, Paul) immediately began backing away from the 18 month deadline, while the President remained stolidly adamant about the entire mess. One can just imagine how the Taliban and other Afghanistan Terrorist Groups are now in earnest preparation for their new "major campaign" to begin in 18 months.

The Environmentalist's Hallelujah Chorus

As most of America now sits locked in the "Icy Grip" of "Global Warming" under a heavy mantle of very early snow, you may have noted that there seems to be a stir in the world's collective consciousness of something more entirely different than anything we have seen before. It took us awhile, but it finally dawned on us...

Religions and Faiths of the World take heed! You now have a new competitor in the form of a budding religion, and it would seem that this new faith is bringing some serious moxie to the table. This New World Order is making a grand effort at being officially sanctioned and backed by the United Nations, Sovereign Governments, Environmentalists and even State-Supported-Scientists, as well as most Left-Leaning-Ideologues. I suppose we can all call this order the "Anthropomorphic Global Warming Sect" until such time as the High Priests can decide on an official name (we will keep you posted).

Why do we refer to this as a new religion? Well, the answer might be a bit more obvious than you might think. A religion is defined in the Merriam-Webster dictionary as follows:

re-li-gion

1 a: The state of a religious < a nun in her 20th year of religion > b (1) The service or worship of God or

the supernatural (2) commitment or devotion to religious faith or observance

2 : a personal set or institutionalized system of religious attitudes, beliefs or practices

3 : archaic: scrupulous conformity: Conscientiousness

4 : a cause, principle, or system of beliefs held to with ardor and faith

Defining the Faith

When we look at definition (1 a), we see what could be said to be a more traditional set of beliefs that point to a service or worship of God. Many hardcore environmentalists view the earth and our environment as if it were a God. This treatment was, in our ancient past, called Pantheism, or worship of nature, and there are still Pantheists of one form or another active in modern day. As we move further down into the expanded definitions we begin to see, even more, how the AGW's (Anthropomorphic Global Warmers) start matching up even better in this regard.

When we look at the second definition we begin to see how our "faithful" AGW's are beginning to conform to certain religious principles. You see, the Warmers seem to believe quite ardently in their contention of man-made global warming in the form of their attitudes, i.e. constantly studying the precepts of their religion—that being rising temperatures as induced by Man around the globe, their ongoing practices, which primarily involve trying to coerce others into adhering to their beliefs while laying down dogma designed to both further their own aims and to isolate and belittle those whom do not believe in their faith.

Also, like many more ancient religions, this new religion requires all of us to participate in the form of alms or tithes to be paid directly to the Treasurer, which would be your National Government as it currently stands. Interestingly, from all the evidence that we have been able to see, the tithe would seem to approach the same tithe as my protestant church upbringing and beyond— that being 10% after all is said and done and after our forced tithes have been fully realized with regard to both individual and industrial economic impact.

Under (3), the archaic seems to match just as precisely as any other faith or religion you might wish to name in the form of their scrupulous conformity and the unceasing stream of conscientiousness that these AGW believers exude in their undaunted beliefs, in addition to their reverential treatment of said religion's titular heads.

Finally, under (4), a cause, principle, or system of beliefs held to with ardor and faith. Well, for Heaven's sake!

Can anyone deny that the Warmers do not have extreme and unshakable faith in their new cause? This despite all evidence to the contrary with regard to these vapid folk being aware of the problems within their religious studies which—at this writing—seems to be in some artifactual trouble—their already having "defrocked" a number of high priests for showing heretical weakness in the form of being unable to hide the "actual" facts gathered and hidden but then unveiled by none other than a heretic (i.e. leaker or hacker) who exposed their illegitimate facts to the world.

Restraint, Faith, and Doom

Our analysis would be incomplete if we did not reveal the etymology of the actual word "religion," which is derived from the Latin word "religare" meaning **"to restrain or tie back."** Now can anyone not see that the entire preface of these Warmers is to restrain or tie back the world in the form of Cap and Trade taxes, carbon offsets and the likes of control which we have never before seen?

However, our observation should also look at the word which seems to be constantly surfacing throughout our initial explanation. The word faith means, among several definitions, the following: **"Faith" b (1): firm belief in something of which there is no proof; (2) complete trust**." Now, can anyone doubt that the entire planet is being asked to believe in global warming based upon unproven evidence? The President and a large sector of world leaders seem to believe in warming despite an equal (if not more) number of Scientists and Meteorologists from all over the world standing up and declaring that "This is not true Science." The President, it should be noted, seems easily drawn to faiths of dubious origin when one looks at the teachings of the Reverend Wright—whom Obama formerly referred to as a "Mentor."

The piece de resistance, in our contention here at Conservative Refocus, seems to finally lock all of the pieces of the puzzle together. What religion would be complete without **DOOM?** Yes, indeed and we have it here. As with most accepted religions, the consequences of sin will be meted out by the deity… and Holy Smoke! Does this one ever have doom written all over it.

We have been horrified with tales of drowning by rising seas, parched ground that will not even grow grass, starvation scenarios, plagues and even the hysteria-inducing fact that only 10% will survive if the precepts of this religion follow through to their completion in the form of a finally realized FOUR degrees Celsius sustained increase in temperature. Where is that darned comet tale (replete with spaceship) when you need it?

First Council of Copenhagen (Why not Nicaea)?

So, even the Apocalypse is included within this religion. The Bible of this religion is not yet available to date as it has not been properly assimilated into the final codex which will, rather predictably, be a stream of digital equations representing both the origins of the past and prophesy for the future—unless, of course, Man makes an extreme sacrifice to this new God in the form of certain luxuries and perhaps a healthy dose of depravation just to make it all nice and tidy. But we are certain that this initial World Summit at Copenhagen will be considered in the same vein of importance as the Council of Nicaea is now with regard to the origins of their Holy Book—as opposed to OURS.

The one incongruous point in all of this is that it seems quite out of character for the Democrats and the scientists to be zealously mixing their Global Warming Religion with matters of the State. As a matter of fact, this is unconstitutional as the Government can "make no laws as it respects religion." Hmm...this brings up all sorts of interesting quandaries as we try to pull these ideas out into the light. If this were not so laughably ridiculous it "might" be more alarming. But ridiculous is so "de rigueur" these days.

The one truth that we should all remember is that within each generation we seem to stumble upon

revelations to our collective knowledge that often prove how pitifully ignorant we were within the previous generation.

The knowledge and beliefs previously held by Man that seemed beyond reproof at the time of their essence often become laughable after later discernment by progenies.

Facts Are Stubborn Things: Rebuttal to Ellen Goodman's Article "My strange and lingering attachment to the facts"

Week of 12/13/2009

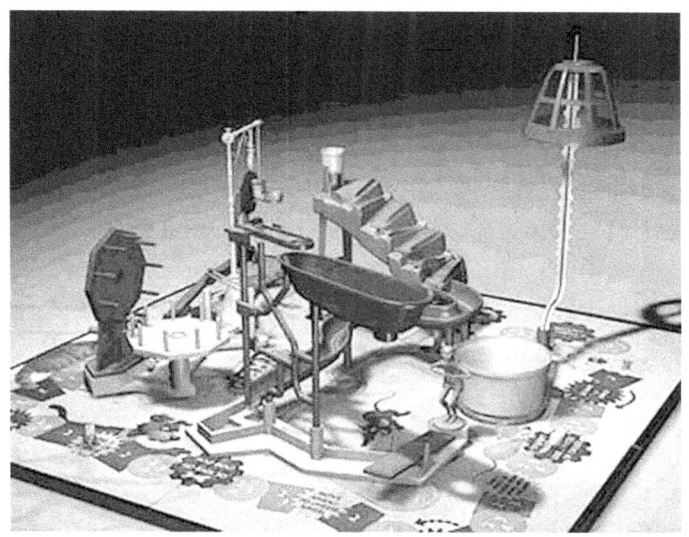

Image 34

Strange indeed, Ms. Goodman! Such a shining example of the misguided and rampant Liberalism both in the media and displayed in your column deserves ample time, space and a bit of work in pointing out such profligate argumentative speciousness.

Ms. Goodman's attachment to the facts most likely refers only to the ones which the Mainstream Media selectively reports (after heavy editing). Her initial thrust refers to an email she received from an individual who was castigating her for the extreme bias that exists in the Mainstream Media. Ms. Goodman then goes on to ruminate about a story posted by an unrevealed Right-Wing blogger in which Bill Ayers was identified to be the ghost writer for Barak Obama's book <u>Dreams From My Father</u>. She states that this particular myth has been "careening" around the internet for some time and was then brought back to life by the blogger who confronted Ayers in an airport where Ayer's then, apparently in a fit of sarcasm, disingenuously admitted to writing the book—noting that if it can be proven he could then split the royalties with the blogger.

Lack of a Sense of Humor? Not Us!

Her next statement points to a lack of a sense of humor among bloggers (she apparently has not visited the Conservative Refocus website). She then goes on to point out that the rumor concerning the authorship of the book in question ranks right up there with the myth that Obama was born in Kenya. Oh! So then, one supposes, it actually does deserve more attention? Well, Ms. Goodman, if indeed you feel this way, you might consider explaining why the Press has not thoughtfully provided us with a copy of said birth certificate? Maybe he was—maybe he wasn't; however, one can only ask Ms. Goodman if she has seen the birth certificate in question? If not, then the question could be considered to be valid until such time as it has been answered and finally laid to rest. The Media now automatically classifies soooo many government proclamations as "fact" without actually fact-checking them that they have nearly, if not certainly, made themselves a figurative "ironic bullhorn" for the political Left.

This fact can be seen in the extreme deficit-laden "air-pocket" that most Left-leaning newspapers now find themselves caught up in with regard to declining readership and revenues. However, the Media does fact check political skits concerning the Obama administration as was the case in a particular "Saturday Night Live" comedy skit. The Media also fact checks books by individuals who, while political figures, cannot pass even a tittle of legislation—referring to the Press's assigning 11 reporters to fact check former Governor Palin's recent book. And yet, where is the fact check of Dreams From My Father, Madam?

Along with many members of the Mainstream Media— Ms. Goodman considers a thoughtful question that has been hounding the President since even before he came into office to be "out-of-bounds." This despite the Media's incessant braying about former President Bush's military records (among many other items too numerous to count) during most of his tenure in office. I wonder if Goodman considered the aforesaid particular Bush story as also belonging to the "fantasy category?" By her "self-delegitimizing" the Ayer's authorship question to the same category of myths as the "birth certificate question," my own skepticism has now been refreshed about the authorship of the book—not that I truly care. Who can truthfully blame Ayers for not laying claim to the writing of this particular book—it should be noted.

Fuzzy Obamacare, Beck and Jail-time

Goodman then goes on to rant about Glenn Beck's assertion that under current iterations of the "Obamacare plan"—which would refer to the bill currently being stitched up in the Senate—you could either buy coverage or go to jail. She also points up Governor Palin's contention concerning the "death panels" regarding the earlier "death planning" entry by previous bills. Well, first of all, Ms. Goodman, it was not just Glenn Beck and Sarah Palin voicing concern about either of those items. It was a host of Senators, Congressmen, legitimate news outlets and most intelligent Americans. I suppose this actually refers to anyone who does not work in State-run Media newsrooms, for Heaven's sake.

Ms. Goodman, can you not lay the crossword puzzles and warm, fuzzy stuff down for a moment and maybe *actually read* excerpts from these bills, please?

Goodman makes a rather feeble, if not vain effort, to discredit individuals who actually "DO" concern themselves with what their government is up to.

Here is the excerpt within the Healthcare Bill in question concerning the "From No Healthcare to Jail" provision:

Willful failure to comply with the individual mandates of H.R. 3962 will be penalized through enforcement of the following Internal Revenue Code:

H.R. 3962 provides that an individual (or a husband and wife in the case of a joint return) who does not, at any time during the taxable year, maintain acceptable health insurance coverage for himself or herself and each of his or her qualifying children is subject to an additional tax. [Page 1]

…

If the government determines that the taxpayer's unpaid tax liability results from willful behavior, the following penalties could apply… [Page 2]

…

Prosecution is authorized under the Code for a variety of offenses. Depending on the level of the noncompliance, the following penalties could apply to an individual:

Title 26 > Subtitle F > Chapter 75 > Subchapter A> Part I: Section 7203: misdemeanor willful failure to pay is punishable by a fine of up to $25,000 and/or imprisonment of up to one year.

Title 26 > Subtitle F > Chapter 75 > Subchapter A> Part I: Section 7201: felony willful evasion is punishable by a fine of up to $250,000 and/or imprisonment of up to five years. [Page 3]

It must be noted that in order to ferret out the above items within the existing Senate Bill, our Researcher and Producer, Kim Stallings states that it required some considerable effort to navigate the "Rube Goldberg"-style maze that is this particular bill—all while she built a commercial website, pulled additional research on an article and filed her nails as well (perhaps). So we can certainly understand why Goodman failed to do this bit of journalistic heavy lifting.

Regardless--our Researcher states that the bill appears to be modeled on the same premise as a game from her childhood called "Mousetrap," where one makes several moves on a board that has a framework of chutes and ladders and other interesting devices all interconnected and built rather appealingly on the board.

When a child makes a particular move they then will often be rewarded with a delightful show of one item tripping another item and so on and so forth which will then trigger the mousetrap for which the game is named. In this particular case, by tripping the "Senate Mousetrap" one ends up in prison where at least the healthcare is, ironically, free (go figure)...

Feel Better, Now? Or Perhaps You Need a Refresher...

So there you are, Ms. Goodman. Do you still feel as if this jail provision is a myth, Madam? Or perhaps you feel that the actual bill is a myth as well. It might as well be, I suppose, in reference to the way you and many in the Media have been reporting it.

The bill actually indicates prison and / or huge fines for individuals who do not participate in this forced legislation. I am tempted to post the above bill excerpts, yet again, in the next paragraph down in the futile hope that after reading them a second time, they might actually penetrate into your cerebellum, Ms. Goodman, and perhaps even reside there in the form of a memory— at least for a hyper-shortened length of time.

The fact is, Ms. Goodman, it is quite obvious that you and your fellows are so busy worrying about the "Right-Wing Ideologues" who have taken up the actual reporting duties of items that may prove damaging to your Left-Leaning cause, you have forgotten that your first duty within the Media is to report the truth no matter how detrimental that truth may be to your flawed Utopian worldviews or anyone else's.

You have just been "fact checked" and your facts are currently in remission. Your self-purported "strange and lingering attachment to the facts," it would seem, is about as useful and effective as chicken poo on a pump handle.

Goodman then continues onward spouting the old euphemism: "You can find believers for anything"—to which I can only say, Eureka! Goodman has just described the exact mindset that the Statists within our government depend upon when dealing on a direct basis with both her and other members of our Mainstream Media—other than Fox News and a few critical outlets. She continues mixing metaphors covering the full range of both the Godly along with the Godless while decrying those whom have a valid opinion differing from her own.

She points up those of us Conservative and otherwise skeptics, along with better than half of the Scientists and Meteorologists on the planet who are not at all convinced of Anthropomorphic Global Warming, as being members of a tribal belief system that bears no consideration. Apparently she also did not bother to read the Hadley Institute Emails that bespeak of a hoax lurking bearishly within the data that only the most devout believers (such as herself) would not consider as perhaps needful of further attention. She then speaks of building facts on opinions when, one should note, her entire column has been based upon ill-critical elitist opinion without even the most meager of corroborating material.

The Bloggy Creek Monster

Goodman continues on decrying Right-Wing blogs while, in effect, pointing up the exceptionalism of such blogs by her continual caustic rant. This opinion-and-beyond website, "Conservative Refocus," was *the first to report* (see "Mainstream Media's Holographic Reality: What Ever Happened to Trust but Verify?") on the actual commanding lead that the US has within its own healthcare system regarding mortality rates using population comparisons—which I should point out—had a staggering number of reads in competition with any other news item printed—and even now is continually being devoured.

The facts within that article are simply unchallengeable as we used the same data as the UN.

Ellen then drags out a Tea Party video error made just once by Sean Hannity while forgetting the lack of news coverage and the poo-pooing by the Media of the countless Tea Parties both all over this country and the huge one in Washington DC—which made the Million

Man March look like a transvestite's bar-mitzvah in actual numbers.

Image 35

Nevermind the exacting reporting by Hannity concerning Rev. Wright, Ayers and Heaven knows what else that the Mainstream Media simply overlooked.

Goodman then points out that internet birthers and the like do not have to fact check. WRONG! *We blanch* at the thought of getting it wrong. If you are taking the time and the considerable trouble to inform your fellow Countrymen—outside of profit or pay, as most do—you will automatically have an abiding need to get "it" right or your time is wasted and you will have little if any readers.... Hey! Sound hauntingly familiar, Ellen?

In closing, Ellen points out how she and her ilk—that have spent their lives in journalism—find themselves and their organizations bankrupt and often worse, bemoaning the current financial condition of the media. Yet we and others have already given her the answers to overcome this problem.

Check out Fox News, Ms. Goodman. Your Right-Wing is our simple truth. We are not insulted by Fox's coverage because it reports everything unbent and "more centered" rather than your constant practice of seeming like a drunk driver with one hand cupped over the right eye, swerving down the left shoulder of the road—often in the ditch or on the guardrail—oblivious to everything but your static-left, worn-out view, while wondering why everything is so rough and getting worse.

Image 36

Your time in the light of pandering a certain worldview has come and gone. Now go and do "real journalism" and see what that gets you. We actually need you but in the traditional sense of journalism rather than as a propaganda outlet. Besides, I enjoy my morning paper and coffee probably more than even you, Ms. Goodman.

You say in your last line that when the reporters go—so do the facts. As John Adams so aptly put it: "Facts are stubborn things." The ongoing financial problems of your news-media driven "collective employers" would seem to indicate that you might need to check and correct your own facts for a time. One has to wonder that if your traditional job had been done properly and in earnest across all sectors then would this financial mess yet be upon us?

The Newest Endangered Species: Al Gore's Credibility on Global Warming, Cap and Trade

Week of 12/20/2009

Image 37

As the Democrats continue their construction of the Labyrinthine Healthcare Bill, which many a citizen is assured of losing their way in, we are now beginning to observe at least one if not more defections within the sinking ship that is the Democratic Party. The Democrats, as we can now see, have crafted a new meaning for the letter "D" that each of the legislators can find at the end of their name in political print. This "D" now seems to stand for "Damned" as in "Party of the

Damned" as they continue to enrage the citizenry. Who would have thought that the cunning and yet bumbling Democrats would figuratively collide their huge and powerful, nearly unsinkable ship of a party into the last remaining figurative iceberg that is healthcare reform? One must suppose that they failed to check the Liberal content of the rivets used to construct their Democratic Congressional Juggernaut.

Image 38

The electorate of the US will now have the task of taking the behemoth, shiny ship that is our country back away from them, painstakingly repairing it, and then relegating the Democrats back to the little blue canoe with which they are so expert and quite so obviously deserve.

Conservative Hearts Afire over the President? Not For Long!

But as the depression inducing intrigue that is healthcare legislation promises to come to the fore in the next few weeks, we must turn our attention, yet again, to the pending Cap and Trade legislation and the events of Copenhagen. Extreme doubt both in our country and in the world has been cast on the global warming debacle that will try to legislate the now economically devastating Cap and Trade Bill into law, and it is obvious that we will all need to be ready.

The President, having delivered his Nobel acceptance speech in Oslo, sent even many a Conservative heart aflutter over the moderate conservative tone that the President used. The Pundits, both Conservative and Liberal, were all fawning over the President's words, which to me, hearkened all the way back to those campaign days that set so many a heart afire. It should be noted, however, before we get caught up in Obama's startling transformation, which was most likely due to a change in speech writers, we should all remember to watch what the President **does** rather than listen to what he **says**. Talk remains, indeed, as cheap as fossil fuels in Saudi Arabia.

Here at Conservative Refocus, our being ever-more jaded at all of the nonsense we have seen spew from

Washington, must include the President's Oslo speech in that vein (The Huffington Post, 12/18/2009, "Obama in Copenhagen Speech: FULL TEXT"). This particular speech was actually more likely a response to Obama's tanking poll numbers than anything else. One must remember that the President and the Democrats are the main reason NOW for our continually faltering economy, increased unemployment numbers, harmful legislation on Cap and Trade, attempts to ruin our healthcare system, outrageous deficit spending and on and on. Once again, the President is suffering from presidential historically low job approval numbers that will inevitably affect his political agenda as these numbers continue to submarine. The next self-serving budgetary appropriation among oh-so-many should, most likely, include a periscope for the President.

clap-clap-clap We Assign the Grade of...Present

We do, smatteringly, applaud the President for making the right decision for our troops, which is the one proper thing we can point to him doing up to this point. However, the President, who has so felicitously given himself a grade of B+ with regard to his presidential exploits thus far on *60 Minutes*, apparently does not read his own tracking polls as they continue their downward trend. In noting the total disregard that 62% of the population has shown for this presidency—our grade—harkening back to the President's days in the Senate—

would be a grade of "present" in the joyful spirit of the Christmas Holidays. The President's Oslo speech—which figuratively was an act of throwing a cup of water on what is the conflagration of Liberal values scalding us all—was nothing more than artifice. So to the few who fell under the spell of the President's oratory skills—we heartily salute your "convulsive fit" of naiveté.

While the Legislators continue busily trying to legislate our healthcare system into oblivion—while also bankrupting the nation via spending—our attention, in conjunction with the President's wasteful Copenhagen appearance, turns back yet again to the award winning Science Fiction which is man-made global warming. The Copenhagen Summit turned out to be a "carbon spewing exposition," what with the melee of private jets, limousines, government junkets and so on. We are certain that the conference did accomplish one major global warming concern—that being the elimination of the carbon proliferating beasts of the field whose lives were ended in order that ultra-fine dining could be accomplished in "triplicate to the third power" at the conference.

In addition, Al Gore, the titular head of Global Warming Science Fiction, as well as our guest star today, made his less-than-stunning reappearance after having cancelled an earlier conference—which mysteriously coincided with the revealing of the Hadley Center emails. The former Vice-President initially stuck his nose out to sniff the air, then catapulted from his 36,000 square foot burrow and started verbally swinging.

A Host of "Inconvenient" Mis-Truths

Mister Gore's vernacular was stunning in its efforts to re-establish global warming's preeminence on the world's political stage. In recent appearances with the various members of the media, the former Vice President asserted the following:

> Gore stated, in response to a question concerning the revealing Hadley Center emails that both hid and falsified data: *"Well, the Emails in question were actually 10 years old"* (slate.com, 12/08/2009, "What in the Hell Do They Think Is Causing It?")

In truth Mr. Gore, the latest emails revealed a date of November 2009. But then you knew that, didn't you, Sir? Were the reporter who asked the question a teacher rather than a host, Mr. Gore would have been excoriated for using the equivalent of the tried and true "well the dog ate my homework" explanation.

Earlier on Conan O'Brien's show, Mr. Gore stated in a conversation concerning the earth and its environment,

"It definitely is, and it's a relatively new one. People think about geothermal energy—when they think about it at all—in terms of the hot water bubbling up in some places, but two kilometers or so down in most places there are these incredibly hot rocks, 'cause the interior of the earth is extremely hot, several million degrees, and the crust of the earth is hot. . ."

The core of the sun, Mr. Gore, is only 10,000 degrees, Sir (nasa.gov, World Book at NASA, "Sun"). We have mining operations that operate far, far deeper than two kilometers down. My 14 year old son would be happy to aid you with many of your scientific mis-impressions. By the way, the molten core of the earth is about 3,000 miles down and is estimated at 7,000 degrees (but please don't reference this article, Mr. Gore, if you decide to use it in one of your books or films...we do have to maintain our integrity).

Ballpark Pranks, Lex Luthor and Prophets...or Is that Profits?

During the recent Copenhagen Conference, Al Gore made the following statement:

> *"These figures are fresh. Some of the models suggest to Dr [Wieslav] Maslowski that there is a 75 percent chance that the entire north polar ice cap, during the summer months, could be*

completely ice-free within five to seven years"
(timesonline.co.uk, 12/14/2009, "Arctic summer
ice may be gone in five years, Al Gore warns.")

The Doctor who Mr. Gore misquotes here later berated
Gore with the following:

"It's unclear to me how this figure was arrived
at," Dr Maslowski said. "I would never try to
estimate likelihood at anything as exact as this."

Mr Gore's office later admitted that "*the 75 percent*
figure was one used by Dr. Maslowksi as a "ballpark
figure" several years ago in a conversation with Mr
Gore." We expect that perhaps Mr. Gore and The
Doctor must have attended a baseball game rather than a
conference and that they were discussing possible cloud
cover for the evening rather than polar deicing.

The simple fact is that the Global Warmers will use the
myth of massive "de-icing" as often if not more
than they use the myth of massive "deforestation." The
Liberals, predictably, will then hysterically run around in
circles, along with the Media, with their arms flailing
around in the air naively exhorting "what are we to do"?
The answer, of course, is to take it to the UN and set up
a summit—which, while at it, should also tackle the
problems of arch-villain Lex Luthor and his domination
of mankind, along with how to get that huge Starship
Enterprise up into orbit without cracking the hull.

In explanation of Gore's constant exaggeration, if not prevarication, about environmental Armageddon, Mr. Gore has thoughtfully proffered this revealing explanation:

> *"In the United States of America, unfortunately we still live in a bubble of unreality. And the Category 5 denial is an enormous obstacle to any discussion of solutions. Nobody is interested in solutions if they don't think there's a problem. Given that starting point, I believe it is appropriate to have an over-representation of factual presentations on how dangerous [global warming] is, as a predicate for opening up the audience to listen to what the solutions are, and how hopeful it is that we are going to solve this crisis."*

The Golly Green Giant

Mr. Gore's Nobel Prize, it would seem, should be celebrating his ongoing Global Warming Science Fiction series that has captivated so many for the last ten years. The bubble of unreality, based upon the above explanation, belongs more to Mr. Gore's vast personal treasure as a result of his Global Warming Misadventures. It is certain that Mr. Gore has amassed a fortune of prodigious fashion as the result of a fawning Media who just want to believe in the religion that is

Global Warming from their "Prophet Plenipotentiary" Al Gore.

Image 39

Mr. Gore's "Green Bling" journey seems to have begun in earnest early in his political career, the former Vice-President having written a book concerning the environment back in 1991 that resulted in a profit to him of $39,000 and then during his year 2000 campaign against former President Bush. After his defeat and Bush's ascendancy to the Presidency, Mr. Gore seemed to naturally fall into the Global Warming hysteria that was overtaking certain "concerned citizens." The former Vice-President made a movie that was a documentary— a huge-scale box office success. According to a New York Times story which ran in July of 1992, Mr. Gore's

personal assets while he was running for the
1976 Congress in Tennessee were estimated at $273,000.

In 1992, Mr. Gore's family assets were estimated in a
range of $153,000 to $345,000 (New York Times,
07/23/1992, "The 1992 Campaign: Personal Finances;
Image of a Wealthy Gore Is Belied by a Net Worth in
Senate's Minor League"). Ironically, prior to 1992, one
of Gore's largest campaign contributors at the time of his
running for re-election to Congress in 1990 was
Occidental Petroleum Company, which employed Gore's
father at the time.

After Gore's campaign against President Bush in the year
2000, his assets had grown to a comfortable $1 Million
(estimated) according to campaign finance forms. In the
following years, the seemingly folksy but financially
shrewd Gore's personal assets hit the stratosphere. In the
years between his campaign against Bush and 2007,
having seen the color of money and the color of ecology
as the same lovely shade of green, Gore began investing
in earnest in Green Energy Technology and the like.

**An Inconvenient Truth...that Wasn't Exactly the
Truth**

Gore released the award winning documentary "An
Inconvenient Truth" in May 2006, which by late October
of 2007, had grossed an astounding $50 million dollars.
When, in fact, shortly after the film was released, a high

court ruling indicated that "An Inconvenient Truth" was "alarmist" in nature and contained nine scientific errors regarding the accuracy between human activities and global warming. Obviously, this particular ruling was even skeptical of itself, for Pete's sake.

According to an article released by Deborah Corey Barnes in July of 2007 ("The Money and Connections behind Al Gore's Carbon Crusade"), Gore's financial investments and connections were heavily focused on Green business ventures. Generation Investment Manager (GIM)—founded by Gore and based in London was one of the largest. This company utilizes funds provided by both institutions and wealthy investors and buys stakes in companies going Green. The co-founder, along with Gore, is none other than former US Treasury Secretary, Hank Paulson, who presided over the financial meltdown of 2008.

GIM is professionally interconnected with Chicago Climate Exchange (CCX), which is reported to be one of the few carbon credits exchanging companies in the US and is made up of approximately 80 member companies which are greenhouse gas emitters.

Goldman Sachs, which is an investment bank whose former CEO was Hank Paulson, purchased a ten percent stake in CCX in late 2006. CCX owns half of the shares of another Green entity called the European Climate

Exchange (ECX). ECX is the European exchange center for carbon credits trading. Interestingly, The World Bank also became a member of CCX in 2006 in order to trade off any excess emissions it might be producing by buying and restoring land in Costa Rica. The World Bank also now operates a smaller carbon trading unit for developing countries.

As a result of Gore's increasingly Green Convolutions, speaking fees and so on, Gore's personal finances have been estimated now in the $100 Million range.

A Non-Profit Group Designed to Lead to Profits?

In 2006, Gore also established his own "Non-Profit" Global Warming group called "The Alliance for Climate Protection." This group's stated objective is to push for more stringent pollution regulations on private industry and to require Cap and Trade legislation in order to force companies into becoming a part of the carbon credit exchange system.

According to US Senate financial reports, the amount of government funding that has gone to global warming research over the last ten years falls easily in the $50 Billion range. While the amount that has gone to the detracting researchers in order to critically verify the data has been only a paltry $19 million. So which team would you prefer to be on?

Gore does not try to hide his affiliations nor his vast fortunes within the very profitable "Green Industry," which seems to trade on the ephemeral, and yet rarely do members of the US Mainstream Media report on this well-known fact. Gore's entire financial spectrum seems to be built on the man-made global warming Industry of researchers and carbon traders so that it should not surprise anyone that Gore is the greatest supporter of the Cap and Trade system that may yet find its way into US law if the Democrats have their way.

What we find interesting is that no one seems to see the gross if not extreme conflict of interests that are at work here with Mr. Gore and yet are accepted by all the nations as business, if not science, as usual. Many scientists seem to be under the impression that no matter what actually causes temperature fluctuations throughout the globe, these variations are but cyclical in nature and will always swing one way or another regardless of man's puny efforts.

Intemperate Arrogance?

The final whimper of an outcome at the snowy Copenhagen man-made Global Warming Conference was an informal agreement by the participating countries that they would agree to hold the increase of global temperatures at 2.3 degrees Celsius. Well how extremely kind of them! Could they perhaps stir up a couple of inches of snow, also? My daughter wants a White Christmas.

God in Heaven must be giggling hysterically at these arrogant and yet clueless government leaders—to put it mildly. Remember, we can't even get a consistently accurate five-day forecast most of the time, for Heaven's sake!

So then, logically speaking, how in the world can anyone proclaim with a straight face that global temperatures will continue to rise or even fall over the next ten or however many years?

Constitutional Onslaught:
The Peril of Unchecked Power

Week of 12/27/2009

Image 40

Yet again, America has come under attack by its terrorist enemies from abroad, this time in the form of a malfunctioning bomb in the terrorist's underclothes that did little if any damage to anyone but the terrorist himself. The Administration Officials, after the incident, repeatedly insisted—rather comically—that "the system worked" (Foxnews.com, 12/29/2009, "Obama Botches Response to Another Terrorist Threat"). We can only (then) assume that their definition of "worked" seems to mean something other than what we have traditionally taken the word to mean—much like "the Stimulus worked" or "Cash for Clunkers worked" or "Healthcare Reform will work."

"Work" to our leaders now seems to mean "unsuccessful effort." Perhaps this is the best explanation for our high unemployment figures.

At any rate, it would appear that our Government's efforts to placate the enemy by arresting CIA Agents and Army personnel—in addition to allowing the enemy access to our court system—and going so far as to offer an extended hand—has not yet proved effective. Perhaps sacrificing a few more of our best and brightest might just impress the enemy enough to make those big, mean terrorist bullies go away and leave us alone.

In other events this past week, as America readied for its "most wonderful time of the year," Obama's elves in the Senate Workshop were scurrying about, even at the strangest of hours, busily crafting what they referred to as the most important piece of legislation since the New Deal. We would agree that it is indeed important but for vastly different reasons. Important, as we see things, would be in its efforts to further weaken our budget deficits, damage our medical system and even hasten the intended rationing of care for our Seniors—which—on that point—one must remember that the Democrats have actually *intentionally done* what they have been accusing the Republicans and Conservatives of trying to do **for at least three decades**.

The irony of all ironies is that if this piece of now-pending legislation were to actually pass it would, inevitably, be important in the exact way that Hurricane Katrina was important, or the Financial Meltdown was important, or the 9/11 tragedy was important; all were "important," but only in their resultant devastating consequences.

One positive note in all of this is how openly if not repulsively the Democrats have executed their sausage-making duties in the prostitution of various Senators by the leading Senate Pimp—Harry "I got your Babe" Reid—in his purchasing of Senate votes by exchanging exorbitant future-cash position layouts from the Government for votes to the affirmative for certain sweetheart states (which held out).

Slithering Salutations... (Oh! And Avoid All Early Tests...NOW!)

Knowing that this violates the Constitutional fairness doctrines with regard to the States did not encumber Reid in the slightest. When challenged by the true Senators, Reid promptly accused them of being "proponents of slavery" and "partisan," for Heaven's sake (Foxbusiness.com, 12/11/2009, John Stossel's Take: "Senator Reid's Slavery Comment"). The fact is that if Reid actually molted his skin on the floor of the Senate and emerged as the pincered reptilian "Kurog from the planet Greazidom" with twitching antennae and all, most of us would be nonplussed—such as have been his over-the-top anti-Constitutional antics of this past year.

Image 41

In fact, the actual rationing of care could be said to already have begun when one looks at the increasingly bizarre revised recommendations by multiple "citizen-centric" health organizations regarding mammograms, colonoscopies, prostate exams, etc. (The Huffington Post, 12/04/2009, "Mammography Debate: Even Physicians Can Get Emotional about Science"). The age-based suggested testing ranges for each of the above tests, screening for the obvious health maladies associated with them, have been strangely and yet revisionistically altered to a substantially more mature age by some organizations to the point that even traditionally Liberal women are wondering what the heck is going on? Are the ideologies doing an extreme switchabout?

Meanwhile, the House Democrats are all readying for the negotiations and conferences for the upcoming session. One can only wonder if the Senators and Congressmen will be practicing "safe legislative practices" by keeping on-hand large quantities of prophylactics for what they seem to be repeatedly doing to American Citizens.

Image 42

On Second Thought...We Now Prefer Boring

As we depart the year of 2009 and warily tread into 2010, we are reminded of the old Chinese insult "may you live in interesting times." While some might find the new paradigm of "instability in all things" as invigorating, most Conservatives seem to find themselves weary of what new and exciting developments will be lavished upon them yet again.

Whether it be some strange new piece of legislation, disturbing news item, or even another economic ill portent, the proportion of discerning Americans who know how things should be, as opposed to the predictable reactionaries in our midst, seem less and less inclined to dutifully bend over for yet another invasively mysterious procedure of pain that figuratively yields nothing more than the words "you may now put your clothes back on" from some disembodied voice of authority that seems more of an echo than a statement.

The incessant stream of intensity regarding economic languidness, in addition to governmental excess, has taken its toll on us all. Most Americans who have stolidly continued their daily work routine, not to mention those who are now yet searching for their "lost ability to contribute," are ever more tensed for the "shock of the day" that must be endured, filed in the "what might this mean" category of their consciousness, and then cheerfully if not disingenuously retort "it's all good!" and continue struggling in a haze of disbelief.

Getting What We Deserve...and Then Some

Unfortunately, we are faced more and more with the reality that "most of it's bad and getting worse in certain areas," while also noting at the same time that the public shift in collective consciousness is one of promise for the not-too-distant future, while still mourning the current state of all things in the present.

The consistent optimist can and will see bright points here and there while still noting the "waxing and waning twinkling effect" of said bright points that they more often than not yield.

To sum it all up as best as one can—most seem to feel that their ideals of what America means to them from their youth onward, in addition to what America means to the world, has now been betrayed—and it only took the Democratically-controlled legislative bodies a scant three years to do the job (plus one new and heavily Left-Leaning Executive position).

Forgiving Ignorance

While noting that the majority of Americans are of a more conservative bent, the Liberals and the members of the Left are all askance at the state of things that remain yet in a form of traditional purity, if not smitten with smugness that we "typical Americans" are getting our comeuppance, and it's been a long time coming.

This unfortunate mindset has often brought to my mind the words from the most famous and influential of all persons in history: "Father forgive them...for they know not what they do."

These people of the Leftward—who seek to change what has been in what is yet the most successful and the most charitable nation in history—are often reviled and hastened to the "evil" category by many Conservative/Traditional Americans simply because the word "evil" is attached to the idea of that which is not good. It is my perhaps naive belief that these people who seek change away from our traditions of Capitalism and self-sufficiency simply do not understand that the prescription for success in a nation's endeavors more often than not requires hard choices that seem to serve liberty at the expense of comfort or security.

Checks and Balances

Does wishing for a new form and structure to a successful Republic automatically constitute evil? My answer would be No—at least not for the utopian-seeking unlearned soldiers of the Leftward. The leaders, however, of such a movement, granted, might be another thing altogether. Isn't it fascinating that ultimate motivation is often the defining aspect of whether or not a thing is good or bad?

The trickery we have seen performed with regard to the current legislative agenda as, in part, outlined in brief earlier, seems to be gilded by a terrible need to achieve legislative finality prior to some future arbitrary date. Many Conservatives and otherwise now feel that this mysterious date is, in actuality, the tipping point of the American populace's knowledge of what exactly is being legislated. Once a preponderance of the Citizenry is in full knowledge of what is being legislated, the outraged cries will be far too loud to ignore.

One part of the Senate Healthcare Bill language (Chicago Tribune, 12/30/2009, "Of 'death panels', and public options") as attested to by our Republican Senators, indicates that the Medicare Panels, that will often determine how and to what degree care is administered, are contained within a provision that the particular section on said panels cannot be repealed nor otherwise altered by any future legislation. This attests to a certain amount of trickery at work, in our opinion, not to mention the fact that such language could render the entire bill as inviolate simply because the Constitution does not allow for absolutes such as this, nor does it historically allow for unalterables within legislation. This lends even more credence to what many have referred to as the "Death Panels."

The thing to remember is that the goal of this healthcare reform legislation has been stated to be, by both legislators and the White House, a concerted effort to make health insurance available to all and to reduce the medical costs of US citizens by alleviating the financial burden that exists to the people, the institutions providing such care, and the Government. In effect, finally correcting a problem (that does not actually exist) within the general population.

How the Constitution Is Shredded with This Legislation

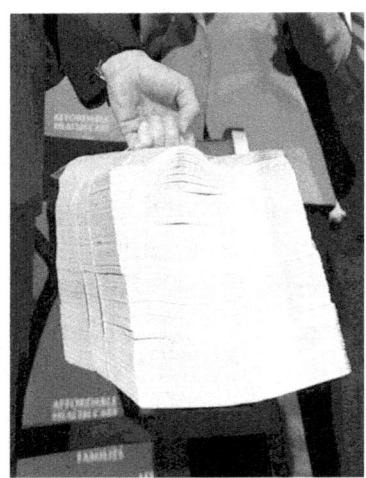

Image 43

The bill, in its stated form, is unconstitutional as it currently stands because it forces a financial instrument—that being health insurance—independent of the Government on its populace, to suffer fines and incarceration. The Constitution in Amendment 9 forbids Government to deny or disparage other rights retained by the People as it plainly states with the enumeration of such rights as set forth within the bill. Supporting Amendment 9, in Amendment 4 the Constitution states that the right of people to be secure in their persons, houses, papers and effects against unreasonable searches and seizures shall not be violated.

The keywords being "persons," in this instance, and perhaps even "papers and effects" in the second. A policy of health insurance would be considered as papers and the lack thereof would, indeed, constitute a crime per this legislation. The simple fact is: The act of living by a Citizen in this nation should not then include a fine against said Citizen in the event that his or her health should diminish to the point of being a financial burden to society due to the lack of the financial instrument that is a health insurance policy.

If indeed various financial burdens, in whatever form they might take, impair a Society—as in the case of health costs—then I would submit that anyone who might require financial assistance from the Government in the form of Welfare and other such financial considerations has now also become the selfsame burden upon Society as the individual who has failed to purchase insurance coverage. By this reasoning, we now can see where this legislation is so terribly non-judicial.

A Framework of Ill-Logic

Shall those current members of society who are insured through Medicaid, and already benefit from various forms of government assistance, be held in higher regard than those individuals who pay their taxes and actually contribute as much as possible—yet are still unable to afford health insurance? Those whom rest on some arbitrary borderline that disqualifies them from receiving Government Aid? Once again, this seems to be the framework of ill-logic that both the Senate and the House are offering as "corrective legislation."

Image 44

The Founding Father John Adams wrote in his "Thoughts on Government" that the happiness of the people was the ultimate purpose of government and that "an empire of laws and not of men" was the true idea of a Republic. He further stated that "a representative assembly should be an exact portrait in miniature of the people at large but it must not have the whole legislative power. For this reason, much like an individual with unchecked power, it could be subject to fits of humor, transports of passion and particularities of prejudices." He held that "a single assembly could grow avaricious...exempt itself from burdens...become ambitious and after some time vote itself perpetual."

His wife, Abigail, in the same instance replied with the following:

> He who is most strenuous for the rights of the people, when vested with power, is as eager after the prerogatives of government. You tell me of degrees of perfection to which human nature is capable of arriving, and I believe it, but at the same time lament that our admiration should arise from the scarcity of the instances.

Renewal or Expiration? Rebuttal to E.J. Dionne's "Finding Meaning in the last decade"

Week of 01/03/2010

Image 45

E.J. Dionne has thoughtfully provided us with his "feelings" concerning the last 10 years in his article "Finding meaning in the last decade," which was published on 12/31/09. The miasma of misinformation was such that we at Conservative Refocus felt it simply must be responded to, as Mr. Dionne pretty much ran the gamut of Liberal nonsense that is salaciously unloosed on a day-to-day basis by the Mainstream Media and others.

But before we get to E.J.'s piece, we thought you might wish to take a look at some of the news items that presented themselves this past week. In the "Global Warming" section, we have news item after news item—both in the US and abroad—of bitterly cold winter weather that has already caused the deaths of many, and we are just getting into winter. The argument for global warming and Cap and Trade seems to be deflating as quickly as Obama's popularity numbers.

Terrorism has been brought front and center yet again in the Government's miserable failure at securing our borders from terrorists. The more we learn, the more we are concerned about the resumption of terrorist attacks that has found its reach to our shores yet again. The Obama Administration has seen fit to blame Bush's Administration for the seemingly burgeoning problem and yet—any fool could see that these events have now started up again only after scant months of Bush leaving office and Obama's Administration entering office. It's not difficult—at all—to draw logical conclusions from these events as they unfold.

Professional Apologists, Cigarettes, Donuts and Soda Pop

The Washington Post, surprisingly, came out in an full-on defense mode of attack supporting the Obama Administration against criticism the publication knew was coming from the Right, thereby proving it is nothing more than a glorified propagandist mouthpiece for the Administration, rather than a bona fide news outlet— among many others (Washington Post Editorial, 01/03/2010, "Soft on Terror? Not this President"). The Post did nothing more than illustrate one of the many reasons for the inception of this website. To the editors of the Post, we can only point out that they exemplify the problems within the Mainstream Media of this country, obviously refusing to question their Government's anti-terrorism efforts despite being a major news outlet whose **reason for being** is to **question everything**. Traditional journalism is, indeed, dead for the most part.

The President, in his One-World Government efforts, also signed away American strictures on limiting Interpol, the world police organization's abilities to harass American citizens. The Administration also, in an apparent total state of confusion, is now wondering why America was so easily compromised by a Nigerian terrorist. This after Obama has severely impaired the Bush Administrations security imperatives on curtailing terrorist incursions into the US. John Brennan, the current Deputy National Security Advisor, has stated that despite removing the military from the terrorist investigative equation and allowing civilian law to take over, the US still has an array of tools at its disposal. I, personally, do not think that donuts, cigarettes and soda pop, or the lack thereof, is going to work very well, Mr. Brennan, but hey! that's just me...

We also have new and even more depressing information coming out about the Healthscare Bill in the Senate which we will certainly address as events unfold—this in addition to Congress apparently allowing Fannie Mae and Freddie Mac to continue to wreak their mortgage-lending-havoc by granting them a blank check—even after they are in receivership apparently for not screwing up enough the first time.

However, since George W. Bush and the few remaining Republicans are apparently to blame for everything that is going wrong in Obama's Administration and the world, we turn our attention back to Mr. Dionne and his broad summation of the evils that have been brought to bear by the former President (and apparent powerful Wizard) Bush by causing all of these bad events to happen even while out of office for one year.

E.J. Searches for Alice down Rabbit Hole: Finds Barney

E.J. Dionne seems to have decided to journey down an illusory rabbit hole in a vain search for Alice as his apparent New Year's "Resolution of Unending Liberal Nonsense" takes flight. E.J. purports that the decade that is the 00's "has been a waste" and in my opinion denigrates every soldier and sailor and airman and civilian whose life was lost in the valiant and so far successful efforts of Liberty loving people everywhere. This not to mention the Twin Towers falling, which marked the exact point where freedom and religious Jihadism clashed and the war of good against unredoubtable terrorist evil began. Make no mistake; history will look back on this period as a crucial point for a multitude of reasons, so that to say it was wasted ignores so many truths that even the shallowest of historical thinkers will bookmark this period as integral in world and US history.

Image 46

E.J. begins his soft diatribe by, of course, bashing Bush in saying that the US badly lost its way by using our military power carelessly and misunderstanding the real challenges to our long-term security. Ok... so E.J.

apparently thinks that terrorists high-jacking civilian aircraft and slamming them into trade centers, defense installations and even an attempt at our Capital itself did not warrant an aggressive counter-strike? Bombing our ships and striking at our civilians abroad was just a slip in the terrorists' bombing techniques? I suppose E.J., of course, wanted to battle these forces with his artful silvery tongue.

He then goes on to point out that our pursuit of domestic policies was a needless constraint on future options and a threat to our prosperity.

Indeed, E.J! If you are speaking of the Democrat's "bright idea" which was the "revised" Community Reinvestment Act's efforts at throwing loan money at everyone—whether they could afford a mortgage or not—in addition to the Government's Congressional wink and a nod at allowing sub-prime lending practices (Barrons, 09/29/2008, "A Memo Found in the Street), then you, Sir, have mistook the wrong "group of culpables," which actually and ultimately caused the financial meltdown of 2008. It has been well documented that the Bush Administration's efforts along with multiple Republicans to quell this conflagration of unsecured mortgage loans in visits to Congressional Committees in 2003, 2006, and 2007, were pushed back by members such as Barney Frank and his like (please see New York Times, 09/11/2003, "New Agency

Proposed to Oversee Freddie Mac and Fannie Mae"; The American Presidency Project, 10/26/2005, "George W. Bush: Statement of Administration Policy: H.R. 1461— Federal Housing Finance Reform Act of 2005"; The American Presidency Project, 11/16/2007, "George W. Bush: Statement of Administration Policy: H.R. 1427— Federal Housing Finance Reform Act of 2007").

That these financial acts of malfeasance were endorsed by the likes of Harry Reid, Nancy Pelosi and Barney Frank, along with virtually every Democratic member of Congress and the Senate, either shows how disingenuous Dionne is or how ignorant he is. The non-validated loans that caused Fannie Mae and Freddie Mac to go under, while pulling the rest of the world's economy along with it, are in large part the reason for the meltdown. The banks that tried to silver coat the "turdles" of mortgage-backed securities into something that they could somehow profit from—or greedily run off with while the house was on fire—only made the problem worse. So E.J., you would then be right about that as far as the Congressional Democrats go. In fact, I could probably reformat your article and cut and paste "Democrats" everywhere you have written Bush and/or the Republicans and your article would be dead to rights.

You have simply indicted the wrong "party of responsibility" whether intentional or not. But then we are used to this sort of thing.

Elitist Apologies: Proclamations of Disclamation and Recycling!

E.J. unheroically then makes a vain effort to disclaim his just-spouted opinion by saying that "it is controversial" but literally destroys his credibility by stating the following: "much of the contention surrounding Barack Obama's presidency is simply a continuation of our argument over the effects of George W. Bush's time in office." What in the holy hell has this E.J. been smoking? To truthfully make an attempt at drawing a correlation between Bush and Obama, in this instance, is nothing but another bold attempt to defend the current Administration's obtuse and ineffective efforts. E.J. is trying to say that Obama's, as well as the majority of Congress' authoritarian grab at auto manufacturers, our healthcare , our banks and many other industries too numerous to mention was a continuation of what Bush started? This E.J. Dionne piece is beginning to look like an "elitist's apology" for the summa cum laude world of "the Liberal now Government," which has already been proven pathetically ineffective thus far.

"The Academic World" meets "Real World" and emerges gasping that their simple equations will not hold forth in a world of complex algorithms. The first thing that students learn when entering real world from bizarro world is "this ain't what I expected." So we can now see why E.J. is following Alice down her rabbit hole, and who can blame him? His effete world of Liberal Academia is not faring well in the real world thus far. E.J. goes on to state that the reason that Obama's efforts at consensus have been abysmally unsuccessful is because of Bush.

Hmmm....I must say E.J., you Liberals have gotten so good at recycling you can now do it with ideas, too! But as with all recyclables, at some point even ideas cannot be recycled anymore. To use your extremely faulty reasoning, we could say that Bush's time in office was so fraught with corrections to Clinton's time in office that he spent most of his time correcting Clinton's errors. Hey! I think we may be on to something.

The Two Liberal Excuses for Current Failure and the Two Truthful Answers

Indeed E.J.'s entire liberal stance seems to be set upon a foundation of blaming Bush, and yet Bush did not engulf the banking industry, or auto manufacturers, nor did Bush run up a $14 Trillion dollar budgetary deficit—that was all Obama's and Congress' doing. Bush also did not appoint an extreme panel of Socialist Czars in an effort to gobble up and command and control every targetable industry in America (glennbeck.com, 08/21/2009, "List of Obama's Czars"). This was all Obama's doing, also.

E.J. then goes on to point out that "domestically Obama inherited an economic catastrophe" and "dealing with the wreckage required a large expenditure of public funds."

#1: Yes; however, we have already shown that the catastrophe was brought about by Obama and others who did indeed vote for the intensifying of the Community Reinvestment Act while he was in Congress and continued his sanctimonious hegemony of said CRA in the Senate. So, in essence, Obama is actually dealing with something that he helped to create, although you will never see him or E.J. admit it—which is why we have thoughtfully included the facts behind our contentious inclusion to the record (see Project Vote Smart).

#2: The banks are paying out the TARP allocation so that money is now coming back to us; however, the massively ineffective Stimulus that has stimulated nothing but our deficits was something that Obama and his democratically controlled Congress dreamed up and then allocated out to their Liberal Pet Projects that does not, in the least, have an impact on the general populace. So, once again, E.J.'s self-serving reasoning falls on its face by shining even a penlight of a beam in it (see recovery.gov).

Deliberation or De-libertization? The Battle for Our Future

E.J. continues on, stating that Obama "is more deliberate in his use of American power than his predecessor was" to which I would say "INDEED." One man's "deliberation" is another man's "procrastination," although we have gone on the record as applauding the Prez for his three month decision concerning the troops. Dionne then states that Obama "does not believe that a war on terror should define American Foreign Policy," to which I would remark that my trundling off to work every day does not define my life; however, it's something that I feel compelled to do. How others view that is their own business. To wit: Stop worrying about what others think and do what's right.

E.J. then points out that the wars in Afghanistan and Iraq—to Obama's view—may not have been the right approach, and that American power was wasted and "dissipated good will toward us around the world," to which I would retort—E.J., we can fight them here in our front yard or fight them there in their backyard— which would you prefer? I kind of like their backyard, but hey that's just me and 304 million other Americans. What do we know as compared to the "Messiah and his Liberal Apologists"? E.J. then rationalizes Obama's stated "disavowal" of victory and overall defeat of those who wish us harm—don't know where I'm coming from? Check out Obama's statement about the Emperor Hirohito and World War II as it regards victory (which it wasn't actually Hirohito)--but hey (American Thinker, July 25, 2009, "Obama on Afghanistan: victory is a four-letter word")! We knew what he meant.

It would seem that Obama only truly relishes victory as it involves himself. Any other "victory" may not serve his well-established narcissism adequately.

Dionne then falls back, in full whining mode, on "Republicans who shamelessly politicize the Obama administrations' incident" (i.e. admitted failure). So, one supposes that Dionne thinks that, as the opposition, we should enable and praise an admitted security failure even after said security failure follows massive US policy changes to previous security protocols? We have learned over time that whenever an apparatchik (thanks Paul) takes the sanctimonious position of bemoaning "politicization"—as Dionne does here—he is in effect admitting he has no true argument.

Dionne then goes on to point up that "the battle for our future will be shaped by our struggles of the past" and then crows about the advances of social (or Socialist) changes in the 30's and the 60's as times of unparalleled social advance. Indeed E.J., but how can you then not gauge that our current circumstances and existing problems within social security and our medical system issues—among many, many others—were not brought about by these "social changes" of which you Liberals are now so proud?

You speak of turning the next ten years of our future into a decade of renewal. We Conservatives are more concerned that you are now turning the next ten years into the decade of expiration.

An Earthquake of Outrage: Government by the Government and for the Government

Week of 01/11/2010

Image 47

As the Senate and the House gleefully play ping-pong with America's healthcare future—Citizens have, for the most part, been frightfully left out of the loop as to what is transpiring in their apparent "demoniacally influenced" Government's legislative efforts. All of this while, many Democrats squirm and fidget and emit howls of protest at what's been let loose in a new tell-all book called *Game Change* (Los Angeles Times, 01/13/2010, "*Game Change* by John Heilemann and Mark Halperin), which is about the often despicable but never boring behind-the-scenes antics of the most recent presidential campaign.

As a result, the word "fascinating" simply doesn't do the current state of events justice with regard to how Senator Harry Reid has described the President as "light-skinned and with a dialect if he chooses to use it," which is an interesting if not veiled reference to the President's possible use of what is linguistically referred to as a "Black English Vernacular." Even more "fascinating" is how Reid, who has been hammering away at Conservatives pretty much this entire year as being "racists" or being "slave-mongers" and the like, now appears **to be the one with the problem**. It would seem that Senator Reid has indeed actually "molted his skin" as mentioned in an earlier article (see "Constitutional Onslaught: The Peril of Unchecked Power") and the true sight of him is beyond difficult to bear.

The Democrats' hypocrisy has never been more glaring than when one compares what Reid said to what former Senator Trent Lott (CNN.com/Inside Politics, 12/18/2002, "Lott: Tripped up by history") uttered in a remark that required "substantial inference" at a birthday party for Strom Thurmond, which resulted in his being ousted as Senate Leader. Apparently racist remarks are really cool and even laudable if one is but a Democrat. WE can only note that the circle of hypocrisy will have been completed if Reid keeps his job. Even Bill Clinton, who is often jokingly referred to as "Black," found himself included in the book for having uttered a comment about "the fetching of coffee" in an apparent racist comment. Whether the Black citizens of the party rally around these beleaguered Democrats or not, you can bet that they will not forget these revealing events.

So, it's OK to utter racially sensitive comments if one is a Liberal and a Democrat? I wonder if any Americans will now be switching their party alliances to take advantage of this new paradigm.

Succeeding at Ultimate Failure

Recent events have also driven home what most Americans have grown progressively cognizant of with regard to our slipping governance. The Executive and Legislative branches seem increasingly, if not haphazardly, more interested in driving home their fallacious and radical notions—at the expense of all—as to their version of America, which apparently includes the word "bankrupt." We have seen massive evidence of this from what the Mainstream Media refers to as the "Fringe Media" or "New Media," such as this website for instance, among many others that have been proven prophetically true.

The Liberal Democratic policies we have been hammering away at for the past 12 months are the same failing policies that have been—ever more –driving our nation into financial oblivion. An estimated one-in-five men of working age are out of work, as an additional 85,000 jobs were lost in December, which speaks directly to the fact that the economy is yet still mired. And until the Democrats stop playing legislative tiddlywinks with our healthcare system and taxes, we can expect more of the same.

We have seen the President renege on his campaign promise to allow C-SPAN to monitor the legislation of Healthcare reform. The President made this promise not once, not twice, but rather an astounding EIGHT TIMES.

So Mr. President--you ask the American people to trust your decision making, and yet you do not follow through on a promise you made to the people repeatedly on at least EIGHT SEPARATE OCCASIONS. It is no wonder that we do not wish you or the current legislative bodies to have anything to do with our healthcare system.

As a result of the President's obvious false promises, normally neutral C-SPAN has come out in loud and outraged protest that the President would use the name of C-SPAN in vain while seeking election only to dismiss the idea in action after having obtained his desired position.

We have also seen that the "highly touted" (Liberal) Stimulus Plan has actually had an even more damaging effect on our economy than leaving well enough alone. The Liberal economic "experts" who have insisted that the first Stimulus needs to be followed by a second—and even more damaging stimulatory drainage from the now empty coffers—have shown how truly brain-addled they actually are. Most of these "economists" have never had to struggle with the difficulties of meeting payroll or paying obscene business taxes. Whereas—in actuality and speaking as a member of the small business community—the effects of a government spending stimulus are now proven to be more damaging than letting things run their course.

I personally have increasingly seen instance after instance of this, after my more than 25 years in the business of various forms of risk management services. Not since 9/11/2001 have we seen the extreme economic upheaval that, in this case, has been wrought by the befuddled Statists in our government. Yet, even then, it was Capitalist policies that freed us from the doldrums.

We have seen far too many homes foreclosed upon, far too many of our friends both in business and personal instances undergoing the dream-shattering effects of bad government decisions, far too many employees losing jobs and businesses shuttering or scaling back. Small business is what fuels America, and our Government has seen fit to bolster the banks and financial conglomerates—which have experienced obscene profits as of late, while dismissively ignoring the country's backbone *which is small business.*

Size Matters (Especially If You Are a Bank or Have Union Members)

During the President's recent grandstanding event of a job summit (Real Clear Politics, 12/02/2009, "Obama & Biden Open Jobs Summit"), Obama actually had the gall to call out small business owners for not freely hiring enough individuals and greedily hanging onto profits (that are non-existent). This while banks have been continually laying off employees on the one hand while accepting government funds—obtained from the People—on the other. Alas...if only Big Business went to the lengths that many if not most small business owners have gone to in order to maintain their employees' incomes—even at the extreme expense of their own.

In effect, the Government has determined on its own that size *does* matter when it comes to the doling out of financial consideration. Heartland businesses that actually make up the job sourcing of real America have been relegated to the back of the line with the vague promise of a no less than *laughable tax credit* as the 'Messianic Measure" to end all ills for small business.

In addition, the Government, it would seem, continually taxes small business and then ironically turns about and gives those taxes to huge corporate entities that don't even truly need the funds, all of which is delivered in the form of bail-out money. Meanwhile we have trucking firms and all manner of small manufacturers and service providers continually going out of business. The true infrastructure of "producing America" is being whittled away measure by measure while financial giants the likes of Goldman Sachs and many others are raking in record profits and bestowing massive bonuses upon employees (yet again).

In fact, when the government "borrows" money from the economy in the form of EXTREME deficit spending—which uses money that is not in its treasury—this leaves a void of funds in its wake that are no longer accessible to businesses or individuals. Remember, Government does not produce; Government only consumes, and the holders of the capital that the Government is borrowing find that the Government is a better payback risk than both business and individuals.

Thus we can see the problem with extreme deficit spending. Were the Government to then allocate these funds back to TAX PAYING individuals and families, the economy could and would be more securely maintained. However, as in this case, when Government taxes funds away from individuals and families and even small business and then allocates those funds to various groups or special interests or non-taxpayers in the form of "stimulus"—or as in this case "payola" to "phantom zip codes," for instance—the economic draining effect is magnitudinally increased.

Explaining... Madness

We have heard some experts even comment on the fact that America now seems to have reached "the apathy stage of a declining Republic" where non-producers vote in majority against the actual producers in minority. This stark possibility is what's driving normal mind-your-own-business Americans into an outraged frenzy.

As more and more Americans who did not wish to believe that their Government would embrace such "funding misadventures" are now seeing the light, a new and powerful "Tea Party Coalition" is coming into fruition. As a result, the "extreme Left" Mainstream Media is responding predictably—that being hysterically—yet again. National Public Radio (NPR), which is a government-funded news organization, in response, came out with a commercial that both vilified and disparaged these Tea Party attendees. What NPR has failed to factor in, among many other news outlets, is the fact that actual Tea Party identifiers include a vast and significant proportion of this nation.

Populism as Opposed to Elitism

The negativistic pejorative that seems to be spewing from these ideological media imbeciles is the recycled term "populism." For instance, "Tea Parties are a Populist movement" is the new Liberal talking point, and yet intentionally negative usage of this comeback term as used by the Mainstream Media.

According to Merriam-Webster dictionary, the word *populism* is defined as the following:

y: [1]**pop·u·list**

Pronunciation: \\'pä-pyə-list\\

Function: *noun*

Etymology: Latin *populous* the people

Date: 1892

1 : a member of a political party claiming to represent the common people; *especially often capitalized* : a member of a United States political party formed in 1891 primarily to represent agrarian interests and to advocate the free coinage of silver and government control of monopolies
2 : a believer in the rights, wisdom, or virtues of the common people

In order to better understand where the "Media Elitists" are coming from, the Encyclopedia Britannica explains "populists" as a 19th century political movement group of farmers, Mid-westerners and Southerners that eventually melted away as a movement.

So, as we can see, and as usual, the Elitists in our midst intend to backhandedly disparage the "less government spending and taxation movement" by branding it with a term that can only illustrate how contemptibly the Media views the consumers of its often ideologically flawed product. As "common members" of the population or "hayseeds," we can either embrace, as we often do, the Media's definition of the majority of the population or we can reject their "label" at every turn by redefining what "new" populism is.

The Groundswell Becomes an Earthquake

What had begun as a groundswell of anger at the Government and its overreaching attempts at forcing legislation that the populace does not support—while shredding and stomping on the Constitution—has now become an earthquake of outrage. Government by the people and for the people seems now to have become Government **by the Government and for the Government**. We are even hearing rumors in the news of outright rebellious protests which "could" cause political headaches; however, more realistically, current political projections now show as many as nine Senate seats could be picked up by Conservatives and a minimum of 30 seats and a possible majority could be picked up in the House.

We have seen verifiable evidence that the Chief Executive—rather arrogantly—will not even deign to meet with and hear the concerns of individual Congressmen and even Senators who are direct and high ranking representatives of the people, such as Congressman Roe, a Physician, and other elected officials (Foxnews.com, 01/13/2010, "Phony Offers from Obama? Or Just Bad Manners?).

We have seen banks who desire to make business loans but cannot due to the boot of newly directed regulators on the bankers' necks (Government again). The culmination of such arrogance makes itself manifest in the President's abysmally low and growing lower poll numbers. Make no mistake; the President's mandate is closely linked to his popularity; as these poll numbers sink, so does the President's command of the legislative direction.

The President's Recent Verbal Slip

When defending Harry Reid's racist remark, the President made a startling admission that few, if any, have noticed.

The President stated the following: *"He's spending a lot of his political capital in the middle of an election to provide health care to every American."*

Now to explain—the President's constant stance on all things Healthcare has been that The People want this legislation and that only the Republicans, for the most part, are blocking it. By stating that Reid is spending "political capital in an election year," the President has admitted that he is aware that The People—i.e. THE VOTERS—do not want this legislation.

Yes, the Senator has spent a great deal of political capital in Congress and the Senate. But by including "in an election year," the President has admitted that he knows and understands that he is going against the will of The People. Remember, the Senators and Congressmen did not elect Senator Reid—only The People can do that. By mistakenly including "election year" the President has subtly admitted now that he knows his legislative plans are unpopular and that—further—he couldn't care less.

To add insult to injury, the above apparently not being enough, the President went on to state the following:

"And that's going to have a great impact on African-Americans and Latinos around the country."

What about the rest of America, Mr. President?

A Democratic Cataclysm: The People Strike Back

Week of 01/17/2010

Image 48

In true "Glorious Cause" form (see "A Glorious Cause: The Return of The True Conservative"), we have seen a bit of history made this week by the people of Massachusetts. After major Conservative victories in Virginia and New Jersey, now we have seen from the Senate campaign in Massachusetts that the American people have had enough of the seemingly never-ending array of Liberal democratic idiocy our Government has repeatedly tried to force down the peoples' throats *by miraculously voting in a Republican after the seat had been occupied for nearly four decades by a very liberal Democrat.*

As indicated in an earlier article, Conservatism and its champions of the past, the Republicans, have once again proved that, even in historically strong democratic domiciles, liberty and Conservatism can take the day. We also find that political "poetic justice" has never been more poignant nor more sweet, than for the United States' (founding) "hornet's nest" of liberty that is Massachusetts to, yet again, 234 years later, send a strong message to those in power who would endeavor to unjustly usurp the will of the People.

The Senate Campaign's snickering jokes from the Media Elite and even "The Meddlesome Messiah" himself concerning Senator-elect Brown's automobile selection of a GM truck would seem to have appropriately back-fired on them all leaving a thin and yet characteristic patina of "oafishness" clinging to each. Perhaps we should not cue President Obama in on the fact that the vehicle company that he heads-up owes much if not most of its thin (at best) success to the pick-up trucks that it both manufactures and sells.

Hearty congratulations to Senator Brown, and we thank him for an excellent campaign and the extreme headaches that he, rather heroically, may have helped us all to avoid. (However, we should only note further that we at Conservative Refocus "truck-u-lently" prefer a Dodge Ram).

The Inept Punishers Play Tic-Tac-Toe with a Complex Economy

Events of this past week also find that the President has now—brilliantly yet again—come out with a both new and exciting idea for the economic doldrums that the US finds itself continually enduring. On Friday, January the 15th, Obama forcefully stated: "We want our money back," and then set forth plans to impose a new tax on the banks which accepted (or were forced to accept) bail-out money from the US Treasury.

While being mindful of the fact that many of these banks are not the innocent simpletons that they often make themselves out to be within this drama, they are, indeed, one of the most important venues for a successful sojourn out of our collective quagmire. While piling money into the banks has had little practical economic effect that any can see, pulling money out of them in the form of "punishment taxation" will certainly not improve the as of yet precarious situation.

Image 49

In fact the "wunderkind" that is our President, it would seem, has never met a tax that he did not love nor a fee that he could not embrace. The true and simple fact is that finding new and artful ways to tax business and then, therefore, individuals, seems to be this particular President's answer to virtually every problem under the sun, the moon and even "Pluto-like" planetary bodies. While we both know and understand that the President's venue of "intelligentsia" is the law, despite his trying to overcome its Constitutional origins at every turn, the President's consistent failures within the economy bespeak of a mind-warping ineptitude at even the simplest of rudimentary financial maxims.

A Legislative Tag-Team of Economic Demolition

Some might suppose that the one good thing about being an American, under the control of the Left-Leaning Democrats of this past year, has had a defining effect on the populace. In our current economic and legislative straits, we now at least have some small understanding of what our brave and skilled soldiers go through. Our lives, in this economy, have been a continual experience of enduring long periods of boredom punctuated by extreme bouts of abject terror.

Truthfully, it would seem that the President and our Legislative branches have been so terribly intent upon forcing their Socialist vision onto our unwilling American system that they have, in many ways, caused the extreme economic damage that is our current state of affairs. The President and Congress shot out of the figurative "Holding Pen" that was January 2009 like a Mad Bull on a rampage within the "Fine China Shop" that is the American Economy. The Statists' smashed into and careened off of the often fragile free capitalistic principles of our nation much like a mad, "bucking bovinic demolition team" of damage.

Whirling and kicking anything that might improve the economy, make a profit, or hire employees yearning for work, the Administration's constant threat of (or actual attempt to) tax anything that moves is what has in part

soured our economy. And if it stops moving, it may well
then winsomely swipe funds from another
disjointed enterprise in order to jump-start the former—
damaging both and only worsening our economic plight.

Then when the bureaucratic rage at liberty and
Capitalism is sated for a time, the Governmental
Beast seems to exhaustively pause, steam puffing out
of its nostrils, while satisfyingly surveying the extreme
damage, the gore of industry grotesquely entangled in its
legislative horns. It then gives ironic lip-service to
how it is doing everything possible to fix the damage and
restore the economy, wash down the over-heated and
sweating leviathan legislative bodies, removing the
bloody evidence of its cause, and then whirling into
bucking action yet again—sparing nothing in its wake.

Car companies--take *that*! Smash those bad
banks...tenderly avoiding only a few; health insurance
companies, you get a special kick in the groin. Auto
dealers...must…obliterate…as…many… as…possible;
mortgage brokers--*skull smash*! Small business? Well,
that's the dirt and scrabble-laden stage upon which the
Beast performs its mad bucking dance of
obliteration....or is it, perhaps, the sturdy foundation
upon which all else is both built and supported?

The Foul Embrace of the Meddling Statists and Their Favorite Pet: Inflation

The one simple truth that the Statists seem to always miss is that the extreme wealth redistribution that they find so endearing and self-satisfying will only cause more extreme poverty, decline, and eventually failure in the end. The free market principles and self-empowering liberties that a free Republic enjoys, while hardy and tough beyond imagination, are not built for extensive Government meddling nor the coddling coercion of Special Interests, and will soon wilt and decline for lack of proper nurturing.

The President who, by his own admission, had stated that the time for partisanship and political grandstanding was over during his campaign and even during his inauguration, has now proven that we should often look at the inverse of what he exclaims in order to discern what events are actually forthcoming from his Administration. In stark retrospect, we have never seen a populace so terribly divided nor a Congress where the fault-line running through it is so easily viewed that it rivals the Grand Canyon in its breathtaking chasm.

Image 50

The leader who was supposed to bring this nation together has now piously split it asunder without even a second thought, it would seem. In addition, never has a forced legislative agenda such as we have had this past year been more intrusive, nor more disruptive of business and the economy, nor more damaging to the constitutionally intoned sensitivity of the American people.

In fact, history has shown us that the man-made national disaster that is our current economy will only get worse by imposing new taxes. While to many the seeming increase in revenue might ease the strain on the treasury, it will actually end up only stunting any growth that the economy might see. Additional taxation will further ramp up the cost of doing business for banks, health insurance carriers and therefore others, and thus the resultant costs will be passed along to consumers and businesses which will then only hasten the foul embrace of inflation that we can almost feel coming.

It's the Economy...Einstein

The President purportedly also has been, of late, setting forth plans (in the "virtual" embryonic stage, no doubt) of helping the tattered remains of small business within the US in the form of tax relief. One can only hope that this idea does not go into the same bin as the "legislative transparency" promise of C-SPAN's monitoring healthcare reform. The relief would most likely come in the form of a silly, weak tax credit for new hires which will end up helping only the businesses who were going to hire anyway.

If I may, what the President needs to be doing is defining new and bold strategies that will offer immediate relief, such as in the form of quarterly FICA and Federal /State tax relaxations for both small business and small business employees across the board—if he is, indeed, serious about helping small business get back on track and get the citizenry back to work.

When President Ronald Reagan took office, the economy of his time was suffering much as this one after Jimmy Carter's four years in office. The problem then was interest rates that were sky high at 20%, unemployment that had peaked at 10.8%, and a dizzying inflation rate of 13% as compared to our current 3%. President Reagan's vision to repair the nation was to cut taxes down to 28% from the high at the time of 37% for most average families and an astounding 70% for the wealthy.

The President had also pared the size of Government back down to a healthier state while increasing defense spending in order to parry back the aggressive Soviet Union, which was eventually contained and economically defeated without firing a shot. All of this caused the 80's to be a time of great prosperity and growth. By lowering taxes for the wealthy, the pro-business President Reagan then excited the wealthy to invest more of their money into the economy thereby "trickling down" the effects of both wealth and growth into the populace. The growth that ensued had a dwarfing effect on any deficit spending that President Reagan had called for in his outrageously successful efforts to grow the economy.

President Obama's regimen for economic repair has so far emulated nothing that we have learned from the 80's and President Reagan. Obama has espoused a "trickle up" economy by either increasing taxation or threatening to increase taxes and fees in all manners, except for the bottom 50% of the population, thereby setting up a scenario in which those who do not wish to produce are repatriated for their non-efforts by those who do. Obama's efforts at growing Government can be seen in the rampant increase in Government employment and pay.

Obama further wishes to swipe into the Government fold 1/6th of one of the more successful components of our economy in the form of healthcare. As we can see, the prospects for business have been gloomy so far, and all signs point to nothing more than sluggish growth at best, which would seem to indicate a certain level of hesitation for business interests to even cautiously embrace the Grim Reaper that seems to be the President's legislative agenda.

Walking on Water is Not the Same as Walking on Fresh Paint...

The true and simple fact is that when this president came into office, the United States had just suffered one of the most terrible financial crises that this country and the world has ever seen. What was the President's answer to this calamity? A Stimulus so filled with pork and slow-moving molasses that it has accomplished nothing but prolonged malaise. Second answer? Cap and Trade regulations and energy taxation based upon a hoax which could only disparage the economy even further. What was the President's third answer to the financial meltdown? Redefining our superlative healthcare system.

Like a poor marksman, the President keeps missing the target! Our economy and the People's well-being and security are the first and foremost responsibilities of the executive position that is our Presidency. The President and Congress have failed beyond miserably at staying on point.

The sad if not depressing conclusion that seems the most plausible of all possibilities is that both the President's and the Democrats' agenda has been one of a severely myopic vision that sees nothing but what it wishes to see, which would explain the state of our economy. This vision, which would seem to exclude all else except the Socialistic mandate of severe energy restrictions and Draconian Cap and Trade regulations, which can only massively increase costs. This vision also demanded Government mandated healthcare which would still leave 23 million individuals uninsured while forcing those who have satisfactory coverage into a one-size-fits-all plan. And finally, an often spoke of vision that is quite pathetic in its empathic desire to be loved and cherished by all of the other nations, some of which wish us harm, but at the possible cost of the security and the respect that this nation has so long enjoyed.

Interestingly, as the dust from the Massachusetts election continues to clear, we are seeing a "singular disingenuousness" among Obama, Barney Frank and many other Liberal politicians now that their "best laid plans" have been dashed on the shores of liberty. Obama has come out the day after the election warning the Senate not to try to jam the bill through until after Sen. Brown was seated (blog.taragana.com/politic, 01/20/2010, "Obama warms Democrats…"), which is akin to a lion warning a gazelle not to run or the poor creature might have to be chased and eaten. Barney Frank has even stated along with many others, that perhaps we have gone too far in trying to push healthcare (nationaljournal.com, 01/20/2010, "Frank: Health Care Compromise 'Dead'"), which is a bit like the legislators pointing a "Congressional pistol" at the American peoples' heads, and after hearing an impotent final click--oops! dud! Saying, "umm....maybe we won't shoot this gun after all."

The Liberal Statists in our government now know that the game is up in oh-so-many-ways and are tenderly trying to retrace their steps backwards out of the figurative room that is our Constitution—where a fresh coating of "Statist paint" has been laid down—as if they were never there. But the stark evidence of their legislative footprints, Ladies and Gentlemen, is everywhere.

We must remember that the House could still accede to the Senate bill and pass the Healthcare Bill that they now have via a House acceptance vote on the Senate bill, to which the American people would simply say to the Democrats: "Go ahead; make our day."

The Democratic Party's extreme carnage that would result in the November elections might be a gentle solace to the Democrats compared to the present-day reaction of the American people.

Regardless....we will Never Forget. Never Forget.

"Ours was the first revolution in the history of mankind that truly reversed the course of government, and with three little words: 'We the people.' 'We the people' tell the government what to do, it doesn't tell us. 'We the people' are the driver, the government is the car. And we decide where it should go, and by what route, and how fast. Almost all the world's constitutions are documents in which governments tell the people what their privileges are. Our Constitution is a document in which 'We the people' tell the government what it is allowed to do. 'We the people' are free. This belief has been the underlying basis for everything I've tried to do these past eight years."

~ Ronald Reagan

Epilogue: Year Two Begins

The Arrogance of Power: An Administration in Denial While a New Leader Emerges

Week of 01/24/2010

Image 51

While Senator Scott Brown "stormed the beaches" at Washington this past week—making his "Everyman" presence known to all—the teeth gnashing and back-biting of the Democrats has been quite a sight to see, to say the least. As the Liberals consternatedly puzzled over why their self-defeating policies have been rejected by the American people, other Democratic politicians, such as Senator Arlen Specter, were busy in other ways. Specter, who switched from the Republican to the Democratic Party last year, accomplished one of

the best impersonations of a Jackass (that *is*
the Democrats' party emblem) that we have yet seen.
The Senator brayed repeatedly in a rather bewildering
manner that Rep. Bachman should act like a lady, while
he successfully established himself as being far less than
a Gentleman as the two appeared on a radio show
together.

We can, however, understand the Senator's grumpy
angst. One must remember that his whole apparent
purpose for switching sides was to go with the most
popular party...*alas*.

Game-changing Senator Scott Brown later made an
appearance that all had apparently been waiting for with
Senator Harry "Please Someone Like Me" Reid. There
appeared to be no love lost when the two sat at a
televised meeting where they exchanged tight
pleasantries, shook hand and pincer, and then departed—
Reid with a rictus-induced smile etched across his face
while he, no doubt, fought to keep from transmorphing
into the evil Lizardman that we often suspect he might
be, whilst struggling to keep his antennae from
protruding. No doubt the members of the Press in the
room were gratified that a terrible reactive explosion had
not taken place such as when matter comes in contact
with anti-matter.

Diminutive Spoor Flies that Stand on Liberal Platforms

Meanwhile, members of the Extreme Left were voicing their outrage at the President for his failure at immediately introducing everyone to Big Brother. One writer who had voted for Obama stated that she had not understood that the "change" Obama kept repeating in his malodorous chant was a euphemism for "Big Government," as in "Big Government that we can believe in" (Nice!). Another Lefty professor obliterated Obama—in language that many on the "Extreme Right" would not even consider—due to Obama's apparent failures at immediately installing every Liberal platform known to man. Keith Olbermann's rant at Scott Brown was of such a timbre than even Jon Stewart hilariously took issue with Olbermann's showcasing an extreme lack of class—if not journalistic insight. Olbermann has apparently decided to relegate himself to the domain of the diminutive spoor fly—to which we can only point out that everyone eventually finds their true place in life.

Not to be outdone, President Obama weighed in to the angst-ridden mix stating, "the anger that elected Brown is the same anger that elected me, and it goes back eight years." In other words, Massachusetts has apparently elected its first Republican Senator since the 1970s because it is still furious at George W. Bush. This would appear to be in keeping with Obama's both frequent and bizarre attempts at rational thought. Obama then, apparently, in an attempt to talk Democratic Senator Marion Barry out of retiring, indicated to Barry that he need not fear a Republican takeover—such as in 1994—due to the following dubious and yet eloquently phrased Obama exclamation: "You got ME!" (This is most likely what Sen. Barry is afraid of, for Heaven's sake).

Obama later attended a meeting in a classroom of sixth graders where, in what could have been a Saturday Night Live comedy skit, a podium had been set up along with the requisite "dual" teleprompters, and regaled the sixth graders to a teleprompted speech replete even with gaze turreting from one side of the classroom to the other...in true "Lord of The Flies" form (you can't even dream this kind of stuff up...).

Image 52

Of Gibbering Statists

Robert Gibbs, the President's "Propagandist in Chief," indicated that the election results were a clear sign that the populace was unhappy with the status quo and that the reason for Brown's success was, indeed, not due to dissatisfaction with Obama, but rather Gibbs stated the following:

> Well, that may be what he campaigned on, but that's not why the voters of Massachusetts sent him to Washington. If you look at an exit poll that was done by the Washington Post as to why they voted, right. So, more people voted to express their support for Barack Obama than to oppose him. His approval rating among that

electorate was 61 percent. Their enthusiasm for Republican policies among that electorate was— for Republicans was 40 percent...

So, if it is at all possible to clarify the above statement...Gibbs is saying that the vote for Scott Brown was a vote for Obama's policies, which is, no doubt, either an indication that the Administration is in complete and total denial of its extreme unpopularity, or it is populated by a veritable host of boastfully prevaricating "Baron Von Munchausens" (you decide). All of this despite Brown's platform proclamation as the 41st defeating vote of the Healthcare Bill—in addition to his stump declaration that the overspending Liberals, along with Obama's budget recklessness, was an anathema. Further Brown believes that terrorists should not be allowed Constitutional treatments as citizens but rather should be treated as enemy combatants—each of these points being in clear and total contrast to Obama's legislative acumen. The Obama Administration is beginning to look like the group posterchild for "Anti-Depressants International" in their total disregard of reality.

Image 53

Catching Crabs on the Potomac

Also, we have the members of the Liberal Media clamoring all over themselves, much like rabid crabs in a Potomac bucket, as they throw out meaningless and ever more extremely spooky—if not ridiculous—ruminations for what happened to (as debate moderator David Gergen referred) the "Kennedy seat" in Massachusetts (with a straight face, too). Many even attacked each other as being mad—if not brain addled— to which we can only observe that Liberal lucidity appears to be dawning—at least on that point. The exchange between Chris "Obama's a thrill up my leg" Matthews and Howard "I'm so liberal I thought the Healthcare Bill was Conservative" Dean was indeed comical. Both argued vehemently about the reasons for the election results as related to healthcare.

Dean apparently felt that the people in Massachusetts were mad that the bill did not automatically gulp down the entire medical system. Matthews—from what we can tell—was chomping mad that Brown took the election (among other things) away from the Democrats. This while some Mainstream Media members, in a squalor of disarray, blamed Obama for not being quite the President that they expected, despite their failure to vet and discover Obama's hard-wired ideology in the first place. (Hello!)

Meanwhile the "Messianic Meal-Ticket's" repeated attacks upon various sectors of the economy, while then pretending to help each back up in turn, is increasingly showing an alarming disconnect at work. The President appears to be adopting the same blocking tactics as a member of the Coakley campaign in Massachusetts which was caught on video (The Weekly Standard, 01/12/2010, "We Report, We Get Pushed"). The campaign worker for Coakley was trying to block access to Coakley by a journalist who had the unmitigated gall to ask Coakley several piercing questions about her election. The strategy, apparently, is for the blocking agent of the campaign to knock the offending supplicant down to the ground while pretending that "it was all a terrible accident," and then disingenuously endeavoring to help the victim back up— only to knock them back down yet again.

The Unbearable Lightness of Being....Obama

The President seems to have adopted this self-same tactic with regard to American Industry. This can be increasingly seen with the President's attacks on "Special Interests" and the like. The President's response to the historic "Democratic cataclysm" in Massachusetts was to come out in an attack on banks and various other sectors, which then, predictably, caused the stock market to lose over 200 points on earnings worries. The Democrats, as a whole, seem to be in a total state of confusion with regard to business in America, which might speak to why our economy is performing as it is.

What many, if not most, of the Liberals refuse to see is that business employs "We the People"; therefore, unwarranted attacks on business in general becomes an indirect and unwarranted attack on "We the People." This is not Rocket Science, Ladies and Gentlemen—to most of us at least. Many in the Media are now referring to Obama's aggressiveness with the banks as "populism," which is the same moniker as they ascribe to others who are in opposition to the incessant stream of liberalism coming out of Washington. (Come on guys…make up your minds; we can't all be Populists, now can we?)

The President and his Liberal cronies in Congress continue to anti-impress most of us in their total and abject cluelessness on how "interconnected" the

American economic system is. The President, it would seem, offers more coddling and warmth to those "individuals who wish us harm" than the employers of "We the People" who are integral to our collective success. In addition, the taxes that the Government depends upon in order to fund its spending largess depend directly on such businesses, and therefore, their employees. Logically, any widespread attack on an industry or sector by those in power can only do harm to the Government's ability to fund its own directives and obligations as a result of that sectors future performance.

Applying Simple Truths to a Complex Position

The President's failure to understand these simple truths has, in many ways, been another instance of his having dragged the economy down for the better part of the last 12 months. In fact, if the President has a "potential problem" with a member of industry, rather than publicly attacking the industry like a hormonally enraged teenager going off half-cocked over something only partially understood, the proverbial Statesman-like President should quietly investigate his disquieted suspicions through members of his Administration and then, if warranted, take it to the People for redress. This President, ever more in a semblance of extreme vanity, seems to take his "unsubstantiated epiphanies" to the People first, then when the damage has been done— whether substantiated or not—the administration zips on to its next culminating awareness (if not grand-standing) event.

The questions that now seem to be floating around in the background of the Nation's collective conscience in this, for the most part, wasted and painful year are just this:

> *What if the President and Congress had gotten to work on the economy and jobs to the exclusion of all else—right out of the gate—and done it properly? Would our unemployment rates have, by now, moderated? Would companies be hiring now? Would the banks have loosened up?*

The President's zeal to put into place an extreme socially left-leaning policy to the exclusion of all else is what has angered the People of this nation. The Washington Powerbase has been casually constructing a new framework for the country while seemingly allowing the old one to burn. The problem is simply that the American people still reside in the old one.

As stated long, long before, this president continually fails to understand that the Chief Executive position of President of the United States is a position that encompasses not just a former constituency in Unions, not just left-leaning ideologues and not just the Democratic Party alone. The US Presidency is a position that requires a specific and singular brilliance in understanding historical precedence and liberty and

how this position owes a certain deference to all—
ignoring at least a portion of the pre-wired ideology that
initially thrusts the individual who becomes President
into the office. Add to this the fact the position of US
President also defaults automatically to "Leader of the
Free World" and it then becomes an unbelievably
complex position that requires *an extreme thoughtfulness
that this president has yet to reveal.*

A New Leader Emerges to Confront an Arrogance of Power

The unveiling of a certain truth to the American
populace is becoming ever-more starkly apparent. True
Conservatism primarily speaks to the overall well-being
and continual freedoms and liberties of the American
people and thereby all free peoples. Liberalism, it can be
seen, is often more concerned with spreading an
ideology of social cultism and governmental excess—
invariably at the eventual if not immediate expense of
the American people and consequently the
free populations of the world.

While America dangles on the socialized-medicine-
tipping-point of the precipice that is a figurative point of
no return, most Americans are now ruminating over the
possibility of what may have been had the President
and Leftist Legislators had their way. The blind trust
that had initially enabled this President has become a

warrant-of-character indictment that the American people may yet wish to serve as the issues play out.

The President's State of the Union address was nothing more than oratorical dysplasia as he alienated both his opposition and an entire branch of the Government—being the Supreme Court—while scolding his own party. Recycling old campaign trail promises and promising a host of new programs invariably left most of America wondering if he actually means anything that he says—based upon our prior collective experience.

But while the pundits and the political analysts puzzle and quizzically cast about trying to figure out who the true leader of the Republican Party is—along with the Conservative movement—we at Conservative Refocus have now identified this long sought-after leader. We have seen massive grass roots movements and various organizations emerge as a compelling, if not powerful, reiteration that can now be deafeningly heard. Not a new party nor a new ideology nor is it a search for new leadership, but rather a mandate of and by The People that those in government must adhere to the same principles to which the populace adheres.

The new leader that has emerged is **the powerfully combined voice and imperative of the American People**.

They will no longer be ignored, which is the way it was meant to be and is the way that it should be.

Image Credits

Forward

Image 1:

"First Year Gallery"

01/2009

White House Photographer, Pete Souza

Image 2:

"For a Limited Time Only"

Photomanipulation, Conservative Refocus

Creative Commons—No known copyright restrictions

Image 3:

Unofficial Seal of the United States' Congress

Creative Commons—No known copyright restrictions

Image 4:

"First Year Gallery"

02/17/2009

White House Photographer, Pete Souza

Image 5:

"First Year Gallery"

06/24/2009

White House Photographer, Pete Souza

Image 6:

"A Stack of Newspapers"

Daniel R. Blume

http://flickr.com/photos/61926883@N00/2054107736

Image 7:

"Patriotic Eagle Head"

Photomanipulation (Stock Images), Conservative Refocus

Creative Commons—No known copyright restrictions

Mainstream Media's Holographic Reality: What Happened to "Trust but Verify"?
Image 8:
"News Journal"
Salvatore Vuono
http://www.freedigitalphotos.net/images/view_ph otog.php?photogid=659

Of Cars and Czars and Credit Cards: Dodging the Wrecking Ball of Debt, Diversity, and Doubt
Image 9:
"Smashing the Bank"
Photomanipulation, Conservative Refocus
Main image by Daniel St.Pierre
http://www.freedigitalphotos.net/images/view_ph otog.php?photogid=691

A Natural Intensity Unfolding: We the People, Politics, and the Press
Image 10:
"First Amendment Flag"
PS7 Original Artwork, Conservative Refocus

Dissecting Liberal Journalism: Is the Room Spinning or Is It Just the Story?
Image 11:
"Spinning"
Photomanipulation (Stock Images), Conservative Refocus

Creative Commons—No known copyright restrictions

A Perfect Liberal Storm: When the Executive, the Legislative, and the Media Enjoin
Image 12:
"Hurricane"
Photomanipulation, Conservative Refocus
Main Image: NASA, NOAA-II
GNU Free Documentation License

The Case for Capitalism: The Statist Menace
Image 13:
"Earth at Night"
NASA, 2/18/2004
GNU Free Documentation License

The Dynamic Duo Rides Again: Rebutting Liberal Columnists in Defense of the Constitution
Image 14:
"Truth"
Author Unknown
Creative Commons—No known copyright restrictions

Part Two: The Case for Capitalism: Attack of the Authoritarians
Image 15:
"Truth and Falsehood"
Sculpture, Alfred Stevens (1817-75)
Author released to Public Domain

The Fourth Estate: The Administration Broadsides Fox News and the Constitution
Image 16:
    "Banned: Free Speech"
    Minishadowlove, 11/11/2007
    Author released to Public Domain

Mainstream Media's Mythos: How Well Does U.S. Healthcare Quality Actually Compare?
Image 17:
    "Medical Ethics"
    Renjith Krishnan
    FreeDigitalPhotos.net

A Glorious Cause: The Return of the True Conservative
Image 18:
    "Christmas Bill"
    Photomanipulation (Stock Images), Conservative Refocus
    Creative Commons—No known copyright restrictions
Image 19:
    "Lumberjack Reid"
    Photomanipulation (Stock Images), Conservative Refocus
    No known copyright restrictions

Fractal Insanity: Political Correctness, the Government, and Denial
    Image 20:
    "Arlington Cemetery"

Photomanipulation (Stock Images), Conservative
Refocus
Creative Commons—No known copyright
restrictions

**An Historical Aberration: From Change We Can
Believe In To Change We Simply Cannot Believe**
Image 21:
 "Resolute Desk"
 02/04/2009
 White House Photographer, Pete Souza

**The Political Richter Scale: Measuring the
Continental Shift in Ideologies**
Image 22:
 "White House Theatre"
 Super Bowl, 02/01/2010
 White House Photographer, Pete Souza

Image 23:
 "Miss Me Yet"
 Author Unknown
 Creative Commons—No known copyright
 restrictions

**Refutation to the Editorial "The Phantom Menace"
by Paul Krugman**
Image 24:
 "Dollar in Chains"
 Jscreationzs
 FreeDigitalPhotos.net

Global Warming Meltdown: An Academian Army of Avaricious Chicken Littles throughout History
Image 25:

"Polar Bear Ice"

Amanda Byrd, University of Alaska, Fairbanks

Author released to Public Domain

Image 26:

"Mount Pinatubo Eruption"

Geological Survey Photograph, 6/21/1991

Dave Harlow

Public Domain

Image 27:

"Diatom"

Hannes Grobe, 1980, AWI

Public Domain

Image 28:

"Ozone Layer"

NASA

GNU Free Documentation License

Image 29:

"Know AIDS for NO AIDS"

Ashvida, 04/27/2006

Wikicommons

Author released to Public Domain

Image 30:

"Deforestation Myth Map"

Wikicommons

Author released to Public Domain

Image 31:

"Global Mean Temperatures Graph"

Leland McInnes

Wikicommons

GNU Free Documentation License

Rebuttal to Thomas Friedman's Article "Some Are Confused, or Just in Denial"
Image 32:
> "1973 Gas Ration Coupon"
> US Department of Energy
> Wikicommons
> Creative Commons—No known copyright restrictions

A New World Religious Order: The Faithful Anthropomorphic Global warming Sect
Image 33:
> "Satellite"
> NASA
> GNU Free Documentation License

Facts Are Stubborn Things: Rebuttal to Ellen Goodman's Article "My strange and lingering attachment to the facts"
Image 34:
> "Mousetrap"
> Author Unknown
> No known copyright restrictions

Image 35:
> "Tea Party Pennsylvania Avenue"
> Wikicommons
> Author released to Public Domain

Image 36:
> "Consent is Silence"
> Tea Party, Washington, DC

Author Unknown
No known copyright restrictions

The Newest Endangered Species: Al Gore's Credibility on Global Warming, Cap and Trade

Image 37:

"STOP Global Warming"
Agnostic Preacher's Kid, 12/20/2009
Wikicommons
Author released to Public Domain

Image 38:

"Sinking Ship"
SS Pendleton, 2/19/1952
US Coast Guard, Richard C. Kelsey
Public Domain

Image 39:

"Gore—Nobel Speech"
Kjetil Bjornsrud
Author released to Public Domain

Constitutional Onslaught: The Peril of Unchecked Power

Image 40:
"Constitutional Onslaught"
Photomanipulation (Stock Images), Conservative Refocus
Creative Commons—No known copyright restrictions

Image 41:
"Alien Reid"
Photomanipulation (Stock Images), Conservative Refocus

Creative Commons—No known copyright restrictions

Image 42:

"Congressional Condom—Ribbed"
Photomanipulation (Stock Images), Conservative Refocus
Creative Commons—No known copyright restrictions

Image 43:

"Healthcare Bill"
Author Unknown
No known copyright restrictions

Image 44:

"John Adams"
Painting by Gilbert Stuart (175-1828)
Author released to Public Domain

Renewal or Expiration? Rebuttal to E.J. Dionne's "Finding Meaning in the last decade"

Image 45:

"Twin Tower Lights Tribute"
Derek Jensee, 09/11/2004
Wikicommons
Author released to Public Domain

Image 46:

"White House Easter"
04/13/2009
White House Photographer, Chuck Kennedy

An Earthquake of Outrage : Government by the Government and for the Government

Image 47:

Photomanipulation (Stock Images), Conservative
Refocus
Creative Commons—No known copyright
restrictions
Image 52:
"Teleprompter Man"
Wikicommons
Photomanipulation, Conservative Refocus
Creative Commons—No known copyright
restrictions
Image 53:
"Crab"
Wikicommons
Stock Image
No known copyright restrictions